Image Profile

		Yes	No
1.	Do you consider yourself a success?		
2.	Do you want to stay at your present job level?		
3.	When you are getting dressed, do you think about how you want to be perceived?		
4.	Do you dress like other women at your job level?		
5.	Do you dress like women at a superior job level?		
6.	Do you feel you look as successful as you are?		
7.	Do others perceive you to be at a higher level than you are?		
8.	Are there other women at work whose style of dressing you admire?		
9.	Do you often receive compliments on the way you look?		
10.	Do you feel comfortable in your clothes?		
11.	Do you feel well put together in your clothes?		
12.	Do you look at other women for fashion ideas?		
13.	Do you read fashion magazines regularly?		

		Yes	No
14.	Do you feel feminine in your clothes?		
15.	Do you look feminine in your clothes?		
16.	Do you wear real jewelry?		
17.	Are your shoes real leather?		
18.	Are your handbags/briefcase real leather?		
19.	Are your clothes made of natural fibers?		
20.	Do you buy the best clothing you can afford?		
	Total		

Score two points for every "yes" answer. Deduct two points if you answered yes to Questions 2 and 4.

- If you scored 36 points, you have a great image. Congratulations!
- If you scored below 22 points, *Working Wardrobe* is for you!

Affordable Clothes That Work For You!

Working Wardrobe

Janet Wallach

Illustrations by Christine Turner

 **WARNER BOOKS**

A Warner Communications Company

To my husband John

Warner Books Edition

This Warner Books Edition is published by arrangement with Acropolis Books Ltd., Colortone Building, 2400 17th St., N.W., Washington, D.C. 20009.

Warner Books, Inc., 75 Rockefeller Plaza, New York, N.Y. 10019.

 A Warner Communications Company

Printed in the United States of America

First Warner printing: September 1982
10 9 8 7 6 5 4 3 2 1

Artists: Allyson Everngam and Barbara T. Sites

Photos by David Neely, Photo Concepts

Illustrations by Christine Turner

Library of Congress Cataloging in Publication Data

Wallach, Janet, 1942–
   Working wardrobe.

   Reprint. Originally published: Washington, D.C.:
Acropolis Books, c. 1981.
    Includes index.
    1. Clothing and dress. I. Title.
TT507.W217   1982   646'.34   82-7048
ISBN 0-446-37253-6   (U.S.A.)   AACR2
ISBN 0-446-37277-3   (Canada)

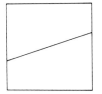

ACKNOWLEDGMENTS

My gratitude to the many people whose interest and enthusiasm contributed so much to the making of this book.

My appreciation and thanks to Kathleen Hughes and Laurie Tag for their understanding, guidance, and good humor and to Robert Hickey and Chris Turner for their artistic direction and perceptive interpretation.

My special thanks to Susan Samuels for her encouragement and support.

My appreciation for the time and valuable contributions of: Lenore Benson, Joan Carl, Barbara Dickstein, Mary DiGiacomo, Millicent Fenwick, Donna Karan, Nancy Kissinger, Hanne Merriman, Nancy Reagan, Dot Roberts, Diane Sawyer, Gail Serfaty, Linda Silverman, and Trisha Wilson.

My love and gratitude to John Wallach for his belief and support.

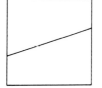

CONTENTS

FOREWORD

Working Wardrobe will help any woman who stands in front of her closet and says "I haven't a thing to wear." What can be more frustrating than a closet full of clothes, yet nothing that works with anything else? Whether for work or for play, office time, travel time or any time, a woman can save time and money if she's bought her clothes by plan and design. And that's what *Working Wardrobe* is all about.

It's a way to organize your clothing to make it work for you,—day to day, week to week, year to year. The key to *Working Wardrobe* is the Capsule Concept, a way to coordinate a number of separate clothing components on the basis of color, fabric and shape. *Working Wardrobe* faces the problem of how to make sense of your wardrobe, how to use it for work, and how to make it work for you. Too many women buy clothing on impulse or out of sheer frustration; they return home with too many pieces that don't work together. *Working Wardrobe* teaches you how to make sense of your wardrobe and buy clothing that fits together like the interchangeable pieces of an interlocking puzzle.

In order to show you how a working wardrobe is used in practice as well as in theory, each explanatory chapter is followed by profiles of a number of women who are successful not only in their careers but in the way they put themselves together. Their creativity and initiative are evident in their dress as well as in their work. All of them see their clothing as a reflection of their personal style. All of them relate the way they dress to the kind of work they do. All of them see themselves as distinctly feminine women. Each woman discusses how she makes her wardrobe work for her.

Working Wardrobe goes beyond fad and fashion and shows you how to get a good return on your clothing investment. It takes the idea of wardrobe building and formulates it into the Capsule Concept, a simple design that saves endless amounts of time, money and anxiety. The Capsule Concept provides a clear, concise approach to dressing. With a working wardrobe you can be ready for any situation and be assured you're dressed for the occasion!

Janet Wallach

Black/Red Working Capsule

12 Pieces of clothing in 2 colors = 48 different looks

		Colors			Will work with
		Black	**Red**	**Accents**	
A. Jacket		Cardigan			All skirts and dress
B. Jacket		Tweed blazer Black/white			All skirts and dress
C. Skirt		Tweed dirndl Black/white			All jackets, blouses, and sweaters. Tweed jacket to make suit
D. Skirt		Pleated			All jackets, blouses, and sweaters. Black jacket to make suit
E. Skirt			Small geometric print, Dirndl, Red/yellow/black		All jackets, blouses, and sweaters. Shirt in same fabric to make dress
F. Blouse			Small geometric print shirt. Red/yellow/black		All skirts
G. Blouse				White shirt	All skirts
H. Blouse				White bow neck blouse.	All skirts
I. Blouse				Yellow shirt Detachable bow	All skirts
J. Sweater			Cardigan		All skirts and dress
K. Sweater		V-neck pullover			Blouses or on its own
L. Dress			Long sleeve wool shirtdress		Jackets, sweaters or on its own
Coat		Belted trenchcoat with button-out lining			

A. Jacket   B. Jacket

C. Skirt   D. Skirt   E. Skirt

F. Blouse   G. Blouse

H. Blouse   I. Blouse

J. Sweater   K. Sweater

Coat   L. Dress

E. **Skirt** Small geometric print dirndl Red/Black/Yellow

F. **Blouse** Small geometric print shirt Red/Black/Yellow

B. **Jacket** Tweed blazer Black/White

C. **Skirt** Tweed dirndl Black/White

I. Crepe shirt with detachable bow Yellow

L. **Dress** Long sleeve wool shirtdress Red

A. **Jacket** Wool crepe cardigan Black

D. **Skirt** Wool crepe pleated Black

H. **Blouse** Crepe bow neck White

Black/Red Working Capsule

Your Capsule will give you enough looks to change your outfit everyday for more than 2 months.

	MONDAY	TUESDAY	WEDNESDAY	THURSDAY	FRIDAY
FIRST WEEK	A. D. F.	D. G. J.	B. C. I.	L.	A. E. F.
SECOND WEEK	A. L.	A. D. G.	D. F. J.	B. C. H.	E. F.
THIRD WEEK	B. L.	B. E. F.	A. D. I.	D. H. J.	B. C. F.
FOURTH WEEK	B. C. K.	L. K.	A. E. I.	A. D. H.	D. J. K.

MONDAY	TUESDAY	WEDNESDAY	THURSDAY	FRIDAY	
B. D. F.	C. G. J.	E. F. K.	A. C. H.	E. F. J.	FIFTH WEEK
E. G. J.	B. D. G.	C. F. J.	E. I. K.	A. C. G.	SIXTH WEEK
A. C. H. K.	E. J. K.	B. D. I.	C. H. J.	E. K.	SEVENTH WEEK
D. I. J.	D. K.	A. C. I.	B. D. K.	C. J. K.	EIGHTH WEEK

Capsule Combinations

A Capsule is limited to two principle colors, each of which can stand on its own or mix with the other. Here are some suggestions of color combinations that you might use.

Black/Red

Navy/Wine

Blue Gray/Wine

Black/Gold

Navy/Yellow

Blue Gray/Yellow

Black/Purple

Navy/Rust

Blue Gray/Royal Blue

Black/Blue

Navy/Red

Blue Gray/Red

Purple/Beige

Purple/Lilac

Blue Gray/Pink

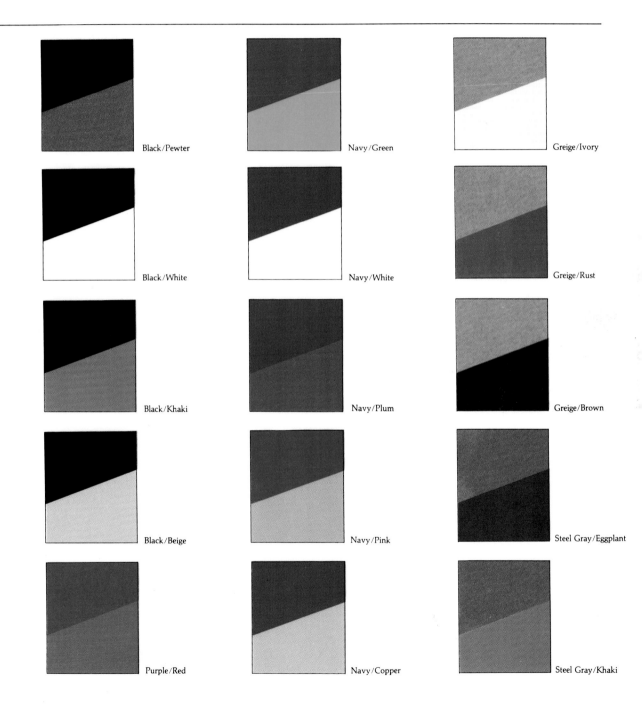

Black/Pewter

Navy/Green

Greige/Ivory

Black/White

Navy/White

Greige/Rust

Black/Khaki

Navy/Plum

Greige/Brown

Black/Beige

Navy/Pink

Steel Gray/Eggplant

Purple/Red

Navy/Copper

Steel Gray/Khaki

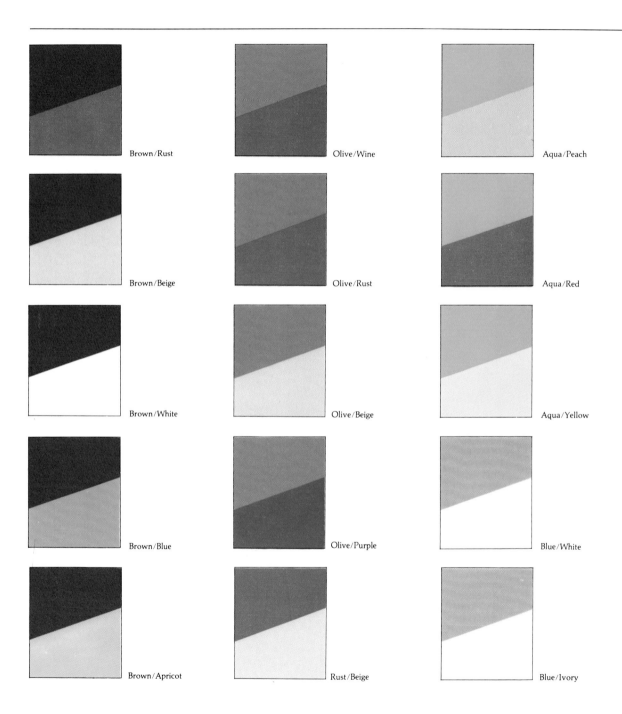

Brown/Rust

Olive/Wine

Aqua/Peach

Brown/Beige

Olive/Rust

Aqua/Red

Brown/White

Olive/Beige

Aqua/Yellow

Brown/Blue

Olive/Purple

Blue/White

Brown/Apricot

Rust/Beige

Blue/Ivory

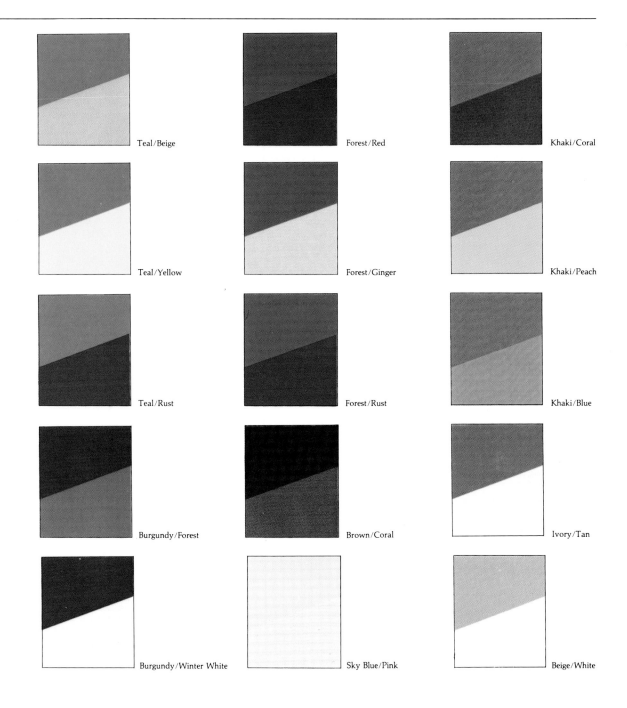

Teal/Beige

Forest/Red

Khaki/Coral

Teal/Yellow

Forest/Ginger

Khaki/Peach

Teal/Rust

Forest/Rust

Khaki/Blue

Burgundy/Forest

Brown/Coral

Ivory/Tan

Burgundy/Winter White

Sky Blue/Pink

Beige/White

Gray/Brown Working Capsule

12 Pieces of clothing in 2 colors = 48 different looks

	Colors			
	Gray	Brown	Accents	Will work with
A. Jacket		Cardigan		All skirts and dress
B. Jacket	Cardigan			All skirts and dress
C. Jacket		Tweed cardigan, Gray/brown		All skirts and dress
D. Skirt	Pleated			All jackets, blouses, and sweaters. Gray jacket to make suit
E. Skirt		Paisley print Dirndl skirt Gray/brown		All jackets, blouses, and sweaters. Paisley print shirt to make dress
F. Skirt		Tweed, Pleated Gray/brown		All jackets, blouses, and sweaters. Tweed cardigan to make suit
G. Blouse	Paisley print, shirt. Detachable bow Gray/brown			All skirts
H. Blouse			Ivory shirt	All skirts
I. Blouse			Beige bow neck blouse	All skirts
J. Blouse			Gold shirt Detachable bow	All skirts
K. Sweater			Rust cardigan	All skirts
L. Dress		Shirtdress		All jackets and cardigan sweater and on its own.
Coat		Quilted		

A. Jacket
B. Jacket C. Jacket
D. Skirt E. Skirt F. Skirt
G. Blouse
H. Blouse I. Blouse
J. Blouse K. Sweater
Coat L. Dress

B. **Jacket**
Velvet cardigan
Gray

E. **Skirt** Challis paisley
print dirndl
Gray/Brown

G. **Blouse** Challis paisley
print shirt with
detachable bow
Gray/Brown

C. **Jacket**
Tweed knit
cardigan
Gray/Brown

F. **Skirt**
Tweed knit pleated
Gray/Brown

J. **Blouse**
Silk shirt
Gold

D. **Skirt**
Wool flannel
pleated Gray

I. **Blouse**
Silk blouse
with bow Beige

K. **Sweater**
Cardigan
Rust

C. **Jacket**
Tweed knit cardigan
Gray/Brown

L. **Dress**
Silk shirt dress
Brown

Navy/Wine Working Capsule

12 Pieces of clothing in 2 colors = 72 different looks

		Colors			
		Navy	Wine	Accents	Will work with
A.	Jacket		Cardigan		All skirts and pants
B.	Jacket	Cardigan			All skirts and pants
C.	Skirt	Dirndl			All jackets, blouses, and sweaters. Navy cardigan to make suit
D.	Skirt		Tattersall print Dirndl. Navy/wine		All jackets, blouses, and sweaters. Tattersall print shirt to make dress
E.	Skirt		Dirndl		All jackets, blouses, and sweaters. Wine shirt to make dress
F.	Pants	Trousers			All blouses, jackets, and sweaters
G.	Blouse		Shirt		All skirts and pants
H.	Blouse			Ivory shirt	All skirts and pants
I.	Blouse	Shirt			All skirts and pants
J.	Blouse		Tattersall print shirt. Navy/wine		All skirts and pants
K.	Sweater	Cardigan			All skirts and pants
L.	Sweater			Ivory pullover	All skirts and pants
	Coat	Raglan sleeves			

A. Jacket B. Jacket

C. Skirt D. Skirt E. Skirt

F. Pants

G. Blouse H. Blouse

I. Blouse J. Blouse

Coat L. Sweater

A. Jacket
Mohair cardigan
Wine

F. Pants
Gabardine trousers
Navy

I. Blouse
Silk shirt
Navy

A. Jacket
Mohair cardigan
Wine

D. Skirt
Silk crepe tattersall
print dirndl Navy/Wine

J. Blouse
Silk crepe tattersall
print shirt Navy/Wine

E. Skirt
Silk crepe dirndl
Wine

G. Blouse
Silk crepe shirt
Wine

K. Sweater
Cardigan
Navy

B. Jacket
Corduroy cardigan
Navy

C. Skirt
Corduroy dirndl
Navy

L. Sweater
Pullover
Ivory

Ivory/Tan Working Capsule

12 Pieces of clothing in 2 colors = 49 different looks

	Colors			Will work with
	Ivory	Tan	Accents	
A. Jacket	Blazer			All skirts and dresses
B. Jacket		Blazer		All skirts and dresses
C. Skirt	Slim skirt			Ivory jacket to make suit
D. Pants		Trouser		Tan jacket to make suit
E. Skirt	Checked. Dirndl. Ivory/tan			Checked shirt to make dress
F. Blouse	Checked blouse. Ivory/tan			All skirts and pants
G. Blouse	Shirt			All skirts and pants
H. Blouse		V-neck shirt		All skirts and pants
I. Blouse			Brown shirt	All skirts and pants
J. Sweater			Rust cardigan	All skirts and pants
K. Sweater			Rust V-neck pullover	All skirts, dresses and pants
L. Dress	Shirtdress			All jackets and cardigan and on its own
Coat		Wrap. dropped shoulders		

A. Jacket   B. Jacket

C. Skirt   D. Pants   E. Skirt

F. Blouse   G. Blouse

H. Blouse   I. Blouse

J. Sweater   K. Sweater

Coat   L. Dress

C. **Skirt**
Wool crepe
Ivory

J. **Sweater**
Cardigan
Rust

K. **Sweater**
V-neck pullover
Rust

B. **Jacket**
Raw silk blazer
Tan

L. **Dress**
Silk shirtdress
Ivory

A. **Jacket**
Wool crepe blazer
Ivory

E. **Skirt** Silk crepe
checked dirndl
Ivory/Tan

F. **Blouse** Silk crepe
checked blouse
Ivory/Tan

B. **Jacket**
Raw silk blazer
Tan

D. **Pants**
Raw silk trousers
Tan

H. **Blouse**
Raw silk
V-neck shirt
Tan

A. **Jacket**
Tweed blazer
Forest

D. **Skirt**
Tweed
Forest

H. **Blouse**
Silk bow neck
Forest

B. **Jacket**
Hopsack blazer
Ginger

F. **Skirt**
paisley print
silk pleated
Forest/Ginger

I. **Blouse**
Silk
Ginger

A. **Jacket**
Tweed blazer
Forest

G. **Pants**
Wool trousers
Forest

K. **Blouse**
Silk
Ivory

C. **Jacket**
Suede cardigan
Ginger

F. **Skirt**
Silk Paisley print
pleated
Forest/Ginger

J. **Blouse**
Silk paisley print
Forest/Ginger

Forest Green/Ginger Working Capsule

12 Pieces of clothing in 2 colors =64 different looks

	Colors			Will work with
	Forest	Ginger	Accents	
A. Jacket	Tweed blazer			All skirts and pants
B. Jacket		Blazer		All skirts and pants. Will make suit with ginger skirt
C. Jacket		Cardigan		All skirts and pants
D. Skirt	Tweed flared			All tops. Will make suit with tweed blazer
E. Skirt		Dirndl		All tops. Will make dress with ginger shirt
F. Skirt	Paisley print pleated, Forest/ginger			All tops. Will make dress with paisley shirt
G. Pants	Trousers			All tops
H. Blouse	Bow neck			All skirts and pants
I. Blouse		Raw silk shirt		All skirts and pants
J. Blouse	Paisley print shirt, Forest/ginger			All skirts and pants
K. Blouse			Ivory shirt	All skirts and pants
L. Sweater	Cardigan			All skirts and pants
Coat	Shell			

A. Jacket B. Jacket C. Jacket D. Skirt E. Skirt F. Skirt H. Blouse I. Blouse K. Blouse J. Blouse L. Sweater G. Pants

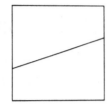 *Chapter 1*

GETTING IT TOGETHER:

The Capsule Concept

Every time you look in your closet for something to wear and find nothing, you know your wardrobe isn't working. Every time you buy an outfit, take it home, and find you haven't the right shoes or handbag, something's not working. If you have jackets that work with only one skirt, skirts that only look right with one top, clothes that only seem to work for the office and never look right going out to dinner, your wardrobe isn't working for you. If you stand in front of a packed closet every morning and can't figure out what to wear, you don't have a working wardrobe.

I have spent almost twenty years in the fashion industry, first on Seventh Avenue as a designer of sportswear, then as a fashion coordinator, and most recently as Fashion Merchandising Director of Garfinckel's a major Washington, D.C. store with an international reputation for quality and good taste. Whether in a store or in a showroom, one technique I learned early in my career is the presentation of clothing by groups. When a designer styles a collection, the pieces are coordinated by color and fabric, so that they work together.

They might include several skirts, jackets and shirts. From these separates, several possible combinations can be made. When the merchandise is presented to retailers, it is shown in the same way. Professional buyers think in these terms as well, often buying a whole group. When the merchandise arrives in the store, it may be displayed on a chrome fixture that allows the customer to see all of the possibilities. She, in turn, might buy a skirt and shirt, and perhaps a jacket. To buy all of the pieces in a group would seem outrageous. Or would it? What if that group were her spring wardrobe? What if, in fact, all of the pieces in her wardrobe could work together? Wouldn't that make her life simpler?

Stores offer many ways to help their customers visualize the new looks in fashion with ads, promotions, trunk shows, personal appearances by designers, and, of course, fashion shows. While big fashion shows cost a fortune to do, more and more women have less and less time to spend looking at outrageous productions of fantasy clothes. What customers do want is to be educated; they want to learn how to get the most clothing for the least amount of money. They want to know how to put these clothes together in ways that make sense for the office as well as for after-office hours. They want to know how to get maximum mileage out of their wardrobes,—what to buy, how to accessorize, and how to update last year's looks.

WHAT IS A WORKING WARDROBE?

Several years ago I introduced a fashion show seminar based on the concept of the Working Wardrobe, that is, a wardrobe that's right for work and works for you. It should adapt to your many points of view. After all, you may be an executive, in addition to being a mother, a corporate wife, a fund raiser, an artist, a theater goer and a traveler. You need the kind of clothes that will do these jobs. At the same time, if you're doing all of this, you are probably short on time. While your mother may have thought it entertaining to go shopping, and meeting "the girls" at a department store was an afternoon's delight, you simply don't have the extra hours to devote to clothes. You need them, you buy them, and that's that. The question is, with a limited amount of time and money to spend on clothing, how do you shop fast, save money and always look good? The answer lies in the working wardrobe. Organizing your wardrobe may take some time in the beginning, but once the initial plans are set, it's simple to put the project in motion.

Fifty percent of all adult American women work full time. They earn more money than women ever have before. They approach work more as a career and less as a filler between school and marriage. They are interested in rising within the corporate structure or in developing a successful business or profession of their own. They spend far longer than forty hours a week working at their jobs if not actually sitting at their desks. When they're out there in the world, they want everyone to know they're working women, making their own way in life.

The Working Wardrobe is geared to these women, to you. It is a concept that applies to any taste level and any purse. Whether you wear clothes by Anne Klein or Evan Picone, high-styled European fashions or basic all-American Preppy, your wardrobe should work for you. You might shop at Sears or you may prefer Saks, or on the other hand a skirt here, a blouse there, and a favorite little dressmaker may be your style. It just may be after reading this book that you rethink your whole approach to shopping. But however and whatever you buy, your wardrobe should reflect a look of quality.

Faced with inflation and an ever shrinking dollar, the best clothing buys are those that last the longest. This may not always tally with what's the latest in fashion, but it makes a wise investment. Think of all those elegant European women who wear classic clothing. They pay little attention to fads and hemlines, and collect only one or two new outfits a year. This contrast always strikes me when I'm in Paris seeing the twice-yearly shows for the prêt-à-porter. There I am racing around town with thousands of buyers and journalists from all over the world, all loger to get the latest fashion message from the newest French designers. Then I notice the well-dressed French woman on the street or in a fine restaurant. And what does this woman look like who strolls down the Faubourg St. Honore or dines at Maxim's? She is very well groomed and dressed in a simple silk dress or well-cut suit. Her age and the age of her clothes are unimportant. What comes across is a feeling of elegance, of quality. She is at ease with herself and comfortable with her clothes. She may be amused by the designers, but she knows what's right for her and she stays with it.

As American women learn to collect their clothes, to buy quality and not quantity, to look for the kinds of fashions that will remain in good taste for a long time, we too are more at ease with ourselves. Many American men have long practiced this idea, always buying the best blue suit they could afford, and always expecting it to last for years. As the price of women's clothing climbs, we are forced more and more to take this same approach. It is the easiest accommodation to our style of living as well as to our pocketbooks. At the same time, we are fortunate to have some of the best designers in the world, plus the ability to produce the greatest fashion at the lowest price. There is a tremendous selection in fabric, color, and styling offered by young American designers. There are great looking clothes at every price point. And that's my point. A good working wardrobe is available to anyone who cares.

THE CAPSULE CONCEPT

As in any other area, those who are successful often have the same formula. The secret of many well dressed women is the Capsule Concept. Easy to digest, clear and concise, it works day and night. What is the Capsule Concept? It is simply the principle of a small group of clothing, coordinated in color, fabric and shape, with all interchangeable parts. Like the coordinated groups I spoke about earlier, the Capsule is an extended set of mix and match pieces, created by you and for you. The Capsule can consist of as little as five or as many as twenty pieces. The purpose of it is to give you as much flexibility as your needs require. The Capsule can be worked around a daytime wardrobe, an evening wardrobe, a work to dinner theme, a work-play idea, a travel package, or whatever your needs may be. It is designed by you to fit your life and your requirements. The basic structure of the Capsule is set, but you choose the pieces that make your picture puzzle a perfect fit.

What makes up a Capsule? Everything you need including skirts, pants, jackets, blouses, sweaters, and dresses. A Capsule is limited to two principal colors, each of which can stand on its own or mix with the other. The shapes of the individual pieces must all work together so that a jacket can be worn with not just one skirt, but with two or three skirts and perhaps with a dress as well. The first step in developing your plan is to figure out your needs. It requires time and patience in the beginning to work this puzzle out, but it sure pays in the end. It may be that you want to approach this in several shopping sessions particularly if you're starting out fresh. But more than likely, you already own some pieces that will work into your Capsule.

Several months ago I was a guest lecturer to a group of women whose husbands were retiring from the military and entering the business world. Both the husbands and wives were enrolled in a course in career strategy. The course incorporated interview techniques, psychological tests and motivational ideas. It also included a session on fashion, given separately to each sex. The women had two interests, one as wives who might accompany their husbands on an interview, and the second as job hunters themselves faced with the prospect of a new position or even the start of a new career. We developed a Capsule wardrobe which could suit either role.

The clothing needs were broken down into three areas: the formal first and second interview, the cocktail/dinner situation, and the casual meetings which might take place. Many of these interviews would happen in different cities around the country, so that a movable fashion feast was required. It couldn't be too cumbersome, or too expensive, keeping military salaries in mind. What was needed were two suits with matching jackets and skirts (one for the first interview and one for the second), a dress that could be worn during the day as well as for dinner, and one casual outfit that could be used for anything from touring a factory to house hunting. This Capsule allowed the women great flexibility so that they never had to wear the same outfit twice in the course of an interview period.

Before deciding on any particular items for the Capsule, we had to choose a color scheme. Dark solid colors such as black, navy or gray were suggested for the first interview suit. Lighter colors such as wine, taupe or camel, or a subtle pattern in a tweed or herringbone, could be introduced for the second interview. By using a solid color that coordinated with the pattern, as for example, a solid navy first, and a navy/wine check second, both jackets could be worn with both skirts. This gave the wearer two matching suits as well as two mixed ones. The matching suits were perfect for the interviews, while the mixed looks were great for any casual outings. To round out the Capsule, we chose a silk shirtdress in wine that would look good with either jacket over it. It was perfect for the office covered up, and great without the jacket after five.

With the Capsule the women were set for a whole round of interviews, both on their own or with their husbands. Many came back giving glowing testimonials of how well their Capsule had worked. They were pleased not only with the flexibility of the Capsule, but many felt that it was their assurance in their clothing that had helped them get their jobs. They also knew they could use this Capsule as the basis of their on-the-job wardrobe once they started to work.

Many other women I've helped have had similar kinds of problems; small budgets, not a lot of time for shopping, and a need for clothes that are attractive and multifunctional. By analyzing their needs and their wardrobes, we were able to develop personalized Capsules.

THE PROBLEM

Roz A. had been a secretary for two years and wanted to advance her career. She realized that the look she projected was not right for the executive suite, but she wasn't sure just how she wanted to dress. Although her budget and salary didn't warrant expensive clothes, she wanted a quality look. Her wardrobe was composed of bits and pieces left over from college augmented by her roommate's clothes which she often borrowed. "I don't really have my own look," Roz explained. "But I am finding that I like my roommate's tailored things, like her slim skirts and oxford shirts. It's crisp and fresh. I was a hippie type in college. Now I'd like to have a cleaner look."

THE SOLUTION

What Roz did have were two good skirts, one a slim charcoal gray flannel, and the other, a wine pleated wool crepe. She also had a navy shaker stitch cardigan sweater, a gift from her brother, which she loved. Working around these pieces, we created a Capsule of gray and wine. First, we found a gray flannel blazer that would make a suit with the gray skirt. We also found a pair of gray trousers to work with the blazer. Then we added a tweed blazer in wine with flecks of navy and gray and a matching tweed skirt. The rest of her Capsule would consist of five blouses, an ivory silk bow blouse, an oxford blue shirt, an oxford pink shirt, a striped shirt in white/navy/wine and a paisley print in wine/gray. The new additions to her Capsule, which she bought over a period of two months, came to $310. The twelve pieces gave her 60 different looks.

Gray/Wine Capsule

	Colors			Will work with
	Gray	Wine	Accents	
A. Jacket	Blazer			All skirts and pants. Will make suit with gray skirt
B. Jacket		Tweed blazer		All skirts and pants. Will make suit with tweed skirt
C. Skirt	Slim			All jackets, blouses and sweater
D. Skirt		Pleated		All jackets, blouses and sweater
E. Skirt		Tweed dirndl		All jackets, blouses and sweater
F. Pants	Trousers			All jackets, blouses and sweater
G. Blouse			Ivory blouse with detachable bow	All skirts and pants
H. Blouse			Blue shirt	All skirts and pants
I. Blouse			Pink shirt	All skirts and pants
J. Blouse	Striped blouse, detachable bow Gray/wine/navy			All skirts and pants
K. Blouse	Paisley shirt, Wine/gray			All skirts and pants
L. Sweater			Navy cardigan	All skirts and pants

Accessories

	Gray	Wine	Accents	
Shoes	Pumps	Pumps		
Handbag		Shoulder bag		
Scarves		Silk oblong	Yellow oblong Paisley square Wine/navy	

To accessorize her Capsule, Roz chose pumps in gray and wine, a wine shoulder bag, and three scarves, one a wine silk oblong, one a yellow oblong, and one a paisley square which could be made into a bow tie, an ascot or a pocket handkerchief. With this Capsule, Roz had a working wardrobe that was crisply tailored to her needs.

THE PROBLEM

Elaine G. had been working for many years, but with her career, her children and her husband all claiming much of her time, she hadn't really concentrated on her own appearance. She bought her clothes on impulse, often while shopping for her children, and what she brought home usually didn't work with anything else she owned. Although she did her work well, she was passed over for promotion several times, and realized that she had better take a good look at herself. "My wardrobe is simply an accumulation of isolated items that have no relationship to each other," she complained. "I don't have the time or the money to go out and buy all new clothes, but I don't feel right in what I have."

THE SOLUTION

Elaine did have quite a lot of things, but she wasn't getting mileage out of her clothes. She had a very well made camel wool suit, and another attractive suit in charcoal gray. She also had a light gray tweed skirt. Among the blouses she owned were a camel and gray small floral print tunic, a white crepe blouse which her daughter had borrowed and never returned, and an aqua silk blouse. Some of the other items she had were poorly made and in shoddy fabrics. These we rejected, but decided to keep the ones mentioned above, creating a Capsule in camel and gray. When I asked Elaine if she had ever worn her camel jacket with either of the gray skirts, she was surprised and answered no. She had never thought to separate the parts of her suits. Since they were made by the

Camel/Gray Capsule

	Colors			Will work with
	Camel	**Gray**	**Accents**	
A. Jacket	Blazer			All skirts and dress. Will make suit with camel skirt
B. Jacket		Blazer		All skirts and dress. Will make suit with gray skirt
C. Skirt	Dirndl			All jackets, sweater and blouses
D. Skirt		Pleated		All jackets, sweater and blouses
E. Skirt		Tweed dirndl Camel/gray/brown		All jackets, sweater and blouses
F. Blouse	Small floral print tunic Camel/gray			All skirts
G. Blouse			Ivory shirt with detachable bow	All skirts
H. Blouse			Beige shirt	All skirts
I. Blouse	Striped shirt Camel/gray			All skirts
J. Blouse			Aqua shirt	All skirts
K. Sweater			Rust vest	All blouses and dress
L. Dress	Shirtdress			All jackets and sweater or on its own

Accessories

Shoes			Rust pumps	
Handbag	Clutch			
Briefcase	Attache case			

same manufacturer, in similar fabrics, they worked very well together, and Elaine suddenly discovered she had many more looks available than she had ever realized. She also tried tucking in her tunic blouse to wear with her skirts, giving a much neater look. Again, this was something she had never tried before. Claiming back her ivory blouse from her daughter was not as difficult as she had thought, and it gave her a versatile top. She did need some more blouses, so we added a beige crepe shirt, a striped shirt in white/camel/gray, and used her aqua crepe blouse. For accents, we added a rust cardigan sweater and one dress, a camel wool shirt dress. Taking one full Saturday for herself, Elaine enjoyed completing her new Capsule. For just $230 she built a wardrobe of forty-nine different outfits.

She already had tan leather pumps, and we added a pair of tan suede pumps. Instead of her beat-up oversized black shoulder bag, we brought in a tan clutch purse and a tan attache case, much more attractive than the manilla envelopes she used to carry papers. "I finally feel comfortable in my clothes," Elaine said, "and I no longer have to struggle with what goes with what. All of my clothes work for me."

PUTTING THE PIECES TOGETHER

Once you are working, of course, you need a good five-day working wardrobe. Assuming that you spend most of your time in an office, you will be surrounded by many of the same people every day. You will probably want to change your look each day for them as well as for yourself. For this flexibility, the minimum working wardrobe Capsule consists of twelve pieces—two jackets, three skirts, four blouses, two sweaters, and one dress. (It may be that you prefer dresses to skirts and blouses, and we'll discuss that later on.) Working with the separates, we'll be creating four suits, three dress-and-jacket looks, and several skirt-and-sweater combinations. Adding in skirts and blouses plus the dress on its own, there are more than enough looks here to take you through two working months without repeating the same outfit twice! These twelve pieces will make at least forty different outfits. The important point is that each item must have independent merit so that it can stand on its own. Of course, the colors, fabrics and shapes must work together for a cohesive Capsule. But one Capsule is all you will need for your working wardrobe. That is why it is important to invest in the best clothing you can afford. The quality of the fabrics, the workmanship and the fit will all pay off. Using natural fibers, such as silks and lightweight wools, will not only reflect your investment dollars in the way they look; they can be worn throughout the year, no matter what the season.

Deciding on a color scheme is the first step in Capsule dressing. Choose your favorite neutral, whether it is black, brown, navy, wine, gray or beige. This will make it easy later on when you choose your accessories and your coat. While some Capsules can be formed around neutrals, others can combine bright colors or neutrals with brights. One young woman wanted a wardrobe that could look very conservative at times, but also would allow her to have fun with color.

THE PROBLEM

When Nancy B. graduated from the University of Virginia, she got a job with a small publishing company as an executive assistant. Although most of her time was spent at her desk, she did have opportunities to meet with writers, editors and publicists. She found that the clothes she had worn in college were out of place in this business environment. "Clothing at school was very low key," she said. "I wore pants and sweaters." Not only did she need different clothes, she also found that she wanted to change her own style. "I wore very baggy, almost masculine clothes in college. But now I want to look softer and more feminine. Besides, my boyfriend says I have a good figure and he complains that I'm hiding it."

THE SOLUTION

In going through Nancy's college wardrobe, several items stood out. She had a heather tweed suit in a gray/mauve combination that she had used for special occasions in school, and which could now become a staple in her closet. She also had a purple shetland sweater and a mauve silk blouse that she loved. She indicated that mauve was her favorite color and she wished she had more things in it.

We put aside the baggy corduroys and faded jeans, and decided to build a Capsule around gray and mauve. We found a mohair jacket and pleated wool crepe skirt, both in mauve, which would give her another suit. She could also wear the heather jacket with the mauve skirt and the mauve jacket with the heather skirt. Then we added a plaid skirt in shades of gray and mauve, and a pair of gray pleated trousers, both of which would work with the two jackets. In addition to her mauve shirt, we added an ivory shirt, a pale gray shirt and a light blue shirt, all in soft fabrics. Her purple sweater could be worn over any of them. The last item she felt she needed was a dress, and this time we chose a

Gray/Mauve Capsule

	Colors			
	Gray	**Mauve**	**Accents**	**Will work with**
A. Jacket	Tweed blazer			All skirts and dress. Will make suit with tweed skirt
B. Jacket		Blazer		All skirts and dress. Will make suit with mauve skirt
C. Skirt	Tweed slim			Jackets and sweater
D. Skirt		Pleated		Jackets and sweater
E. Skirt		Plaid full Gray/Mauve		Jackets and sweater
F. Pants	Pleated trousers			Jackets and sweater
G. Blouse		Shirt		All skirts and pants
H. Blouse			Ivory shirt	All skirts and pants
I. Blouse	Shirt			All skirts and pants
J. Blouse			Light blue shirt	All skirts and pants
K. Sweater			Purple pullover	All skirts and pants
L. Dress		Jewel neck, long sleeves		Jackets or on its own

Accessories

Shoes	Pumps		Wine pumps	
Handbag			Wine envelope	

mauve wool jersey dress with a jewel neck, long sleeves, a narrow waist and full skirt to show off her figure, but covered up enough to wear to work with or without either of the two jackets she had. Nancy loved looking for bargains and bought her clothes on sale and at discount stores for $225.

To give her Capsule a polished look, we rejected the clogs she had been wearing for so long, and chose two pairs of pumps, one in wine and one in gray. A neat wine envelope handbag completed the picture.

Discovering your best Capsule colors can be a new awakening. It may be that you've always worn gray, but this is the time to find the "real" you. Do you feel strong in black, authoritative in gray, or do you feel more sincere in blue? Does your fair skin light up against pale pastels or is the contrast more dramatic against black? Does red make you feel daring or do you feel dominant in purple? Take the following quiz to find out your true color preferences.

Color Profile

1. Arrange the clothes in your closet by *color* only. Include all skirts, pants, jackets, and dresses. Which colors appear most often?

2. Now eliminate the clothes you don't wear very often. What colors are dominant in the remainder of your wardrobe?

3. What color do you associate with each of the following adjectives?

Sophisticated _____
Sincere _____
Boring _____
Conservative _____
Aggressive _____

Masculine_____
Feminine _____
Dowdy _____
Sad _____
Cheerful _____

Now circle those adjectives you would like to have applied to you.

4. If you had to wear the same outfit for three days in a row, what color would it be?

5. If you were invited to lunch with your boss, what color outfit would you choose?

6. Think of outfits you have worn that have brought you many compliments. What colors are they?

7. If you could buy one outfit that you have seen recently in a store or in a magazine, what color would it be?

8. Think of someone whose style of dressing you admire. What colors do they usually wear?

9. Have you recently tried on something, loved it, but were afraid to buy it? What color was it?

10. What color do you feel best in?

CHOOSING YOUR CAPSULE

Every woman who works in an office or meets with clients or other people in business situations needs one suit in a dark solid color. In situations such as conferences, presentations, reviews, or job interviews, a dark suit is in order. A man in a similar situation wouldn't think twice: he'd pull out his good navy suit. A woman must look as sincere and authoritative as her male peers. The basic colors are black, brown, navy, wine, gray or beige. In this case we'll choose black. (Our second color will be red which will be introduced later on.) To start, you'll need one black jacket and one black skirt. Though together they make a total suit, they may be bought as separates from a sportswear department, (in which case make sure the blacks match) or they may be purchased as a unit from a suit or dress department.

The second jacket and skirt may be of a lighter color or in a subtle pattern such as a tweed, herringbone, or houndstooth. In this case, a salt-and-pepper tweed would be a good companion to the black suit. Select a tweed jacket and a tweed skirt (matching, of course), again choosing either sportswear or actual suit components. In making your selection, be sure that the black jacket works with the tweed skirt, and that the tweed jacket goes well with the black skirt. The best fabrics to choose are wool, silk, cotton and linen. All of these are natural fibers which have the look and feel of quality.

The shapes of the jackets may be the same or different, so long as they complement both skirts. You may feel you have greater diversity in your Capsule if you choose jackets that have different silhouettes. One may be a traditional blazer, the other a cardigan shape. One may be a short jacket, stopping at the waist, the other long and to the hip. Of course, they may both be the same style if you feel there is one particular shape that suits your figure best. Shorter women may prefer jackets that stop at the waistline; taller women may feel more comfortable in a longer look.

The same principle applies to the shape of the skirts. They may both be straight and slim, or one slim, the other pleated. One skirt may be a side wrap, the other a front-button dirndl. The third skirt in your capsule can be softer in look and texture. A wool challis in a foulard pattern would add another dimension to your wardrobe. This will also bring in our second color, red, set against a black ground. Teaming this print skirt with a blouse of the same fabric would give a dress look as well. If pants are your style, you might even substitute trousers for one of the skirts.

The most important thing to remember is that whatever you wear, it must look right on you. If it looks great on a high-fashion model, but drowns you out, don't buy it (even if a naive salesperson tells you it's the latest thing). Fashion magazine models are about six feet tall; and if you are five feet three, you'll look silly trying to imitate them. On the other hand, if something looks terrific on you, it doesn't matter whether it's the latest look in *Vogue.* Wear it! The best dressed women in the world don't follow every fashion fad, but build on their wardrobes year after year.

O.K., we've selected the jackets and skirts, and now we need the blouses. At least one blouse should be white or off-white. Just like the businessman, you'll need this kind of shirt with your dark suit for a crisp, efficient appearance. (I'll use the terms shirt and blouse interchangeably, as it will depend on your style, whether tailored or soft, for the look you like.) Your first blouse should be in a crepe fabric, long sleeved, with a notched collar, bow neck or stock tie. Your second blouse may be in another solid color, preferably a light shade such as beige, gray, pale blue, or pink. You may decide to pick another white or cream top in a different silhouette from the first. As to the style, if you've chosen a shirt for your first, you might like a bow for your second blouse or vice versa. The third blouse could be another solid color, or as in this case, you would pick up the foulard pattern to match the skirt. If you choose the latter, it must work with your tweeds as well as with your solids. The right foulard can look terrific with a tweed; the wrong one can be a disaster. This may be a little tricky, and the trained eye of a professional salesperson can help a great deal. The fourth blouse can be a soft shirt style and introduce an accent color as, for example, chrome yellow.

Two sweaters are the next pieces to acquire. The first style should be a cardigan in a solid color. It could be black, gray, brick, red, royal blue, purple—any color that works with your skirts and your blouses. The choice is yours to make. In this case, a red sweater would work with all the skirts and pull together the whole capsule. The second sweater should be a pullover, preferably a V neck or jewel neck that can be worn alone or over a blouse. The color and shape of this sweater should work well under your cardigan and under your jackets as well as on its own. A black pullover can be worn with the black skirt to make a one-piece dress look.

One last piece will complete the picture, and that is a dress. This should be a tailored style, long sleeved with a slim skirt. This very functional dress may have a shirt collar, jewel neck, turtle neck or high V. It should be in a silk or wool, and in a neutral color that will look good under your black jacket, your tweed jacket, and your cardigan. You could choose cream, red, gray, or black, but for this Capsule we'll use red. Again, the most important thing to remember is that you feel comfortable in the color you choose, and that it works with your Capsule. This dress will be perfect at the office, especially when worn with a jacket for business meetings. With the right accessories, it will be great for drinks, dinner, or the theater.

Of course, your suits give you the same flexibility. By simply changing accessories, a suit will take you easily from morning to night.

THE DRESS OPTION

What if you prefer dresses to sportswear? Is the Capsule Concept feasible for you? Absolutely. The key here is a dress-and-jacket look. A simple Capsule-should consist of seven pieces—five dresses and two jackets. Once again, if you are in a conference room, eye to eye with your peers or superiors, you'll want to look as broad shouldered as they. This is the function of the jackets. It doesn't really matter whether you are wearing a blouse and skirt or a dress beneath the jacket. But the kind of dress you're wearing does matter. It should be fairly tailored and have long sleeves if possible. It's easier to adapt a simple tailored style to many looks than it is one with ruffles and flourishes. Shirt-dresses are the most flexible.

Once again, a two-color scheme is important. This time we'll work with navy and beige. Again, the fabrics will be natural fibers or blends of silk, wool, linen, and cotton.

The first dress must have a navy skirt, while the bodice could be navy, white, or beige. Combining this dress with your navy jacket (and again, be sure the colors match) will give you an excellent suit look. You may be able to find an ensemble like this in a dress department. Many manufacturers make dress and jacket outfits, which saves you the problems of matching. The second dress you select could be beige, and again, a shirtdress would be an excellent choice. However, a simple high round or bow neckline would work well too. As a change of pace, for your third dress you might like a small pattern—perhaps a tie print, a plaid or a check that combines the basic Capsule colors. The fourth dress could be in another shade of beige, perhaps in another style. If your first beige choice is a silk shirtdress, the second might be a wool crepe with a jewel or bow neck. The fifth dress might be in another pattern or perhaps introduce a solid rust or copper color.

You will need two jackets, one in navy and one in beige. Your jackets will work over all of the dresses, giving you suited looks as well as contrasting outfits. As with the blue outfit, the beige jacket should match the beige skirt. If they are not a pure match, the colors should blend. The jacket shapes may be similar or different, blazers or cardigans, since both styles work well with tailored dresses. Naturally, the dresses will be fine on their own, and need not be worn with a jacket to look complete.

One woman came to me anxiously seeking help for a new wardrobe. She knew she preferred wearing dresses but wasn't sure she could get enough looks from them.

Navy/Beige Dress Capsule

5 dresses + 2 jackets = 15 different looks

	Colors			Will work with
	Navy	**Beige**	**Accents**	
A. Dress	Shirtdress			Both jackets and on its own
B. Dress		Shirtdress		Both jackets and on its own
C. Dress	Button-front Navy/Beige check			Both jackets and on its own
D. Dress	V-neck, two tone Beige top/Navy skirt			Both jackets and on its own
E. Dress			Shirtdress, Rust	Both jackets and on its own
F. Jacket	Cardigan			All dresses
G. Jacket		Blazer		All dresses
Coat	Wrap reversible Navy/Beige			

THE PROBLEM

Sarah S. had stayed home to raise four children, but when the youngest entered high school, Sarah decided to get a job. With her interest in art, and a college degree in art history, she was hired to do public relations for a small museum. Although no one at work was terribly fashion conscious, Sarah soon found that her job demanded she be at openings and receptions as well as at luncheons with the press. The casual clothes which had served her well would no longer do the job, and the cocktail clothes she owned were too dressy to go to work. What she needed were clothes that would take her from the storage rooms of the museum to lunches and big receptions sometimes all in one day.

THE SOLUTION

Sarah felt most comfortable in dresses, and because she was slightly over-weight, she preferred to wear dark colors which she felt made her look slimmer. She chose a Capsule in black and gray but knew she could highlight her face with brightly colored accessories. She chose mostly jumper style dresses as they could be worn with the blouses she already owned, or bare, with jewelry to dress them up. She also felt comfortable in shirtdresses so she selected two of these as well. The outfit she had worn for job interviews was a black and white checked jumper which she had teamed with a black jacket. She added a black jumper, a gray jumper and a gray print silk shirtdress. She already had a black shirtdress. In addition, she bought a gray velvet jacket which could go over all of the dresses. For $435 Sarah built a Capsule of thirty-four different looks based on five dresses.

To brighten her Capsule, Sarah chose three silk scarves, one in red, one in hot pink, and one in royal blue. She owned earrings and necklaces as well as a good watch. She also had a pair of black slingback shoes. What she did need was a

Black/Gray Capsule

	Colors			Will work with
	Black	**Gray**	**Accents**	
A. Dress	Checked jumper Black/white			Jackets or on its own. With or without blouse
B. Dress	Jumper			Jackets or on its own. With or without blouse
C. Dress		Jumper		Jackets or on its own. With or without blouse
D. Dress		Print shirtdress		Jackets or on its own
E. Skirt	Shirtdress			Jackets or on its own
F. Jacket	Cardigan			All dresses
G. Jacket		Cardigan		All dresses
H. Blouse			White bow-neck	
I. Blouse			Red shirt, detachable bow	
J. Blouse			Hot pink	
K. Blouse			White shirt	
L. Sweater			Yellow turtleneck	

Accessories

Shoes	Slingbacks Pumps			
Handbag	Clutch			
Scarves	Royal blue oblong		Red oblong Hot pink square	

pair of black pumps and a small black handbag. "With this Capsule," she said, "I feel I'm dressed appropriately at my office and I look right in the evening. I can be as dressed up or dressed down as I like."

WHAT ABOUT A COAT?

The plus piece in any wardrobe is a coat. Ideally, it will work with all of your Capsules in color and style. A good coat should go from morning to night, business to pleasure, informal to dressy. Though initially it will take a good chunk of your budget, the mileage you get from it will justify the investment.

If you are buying an all-weather coat, there are several things to consider. First, the coat should fit over all of your clothes. It should be roomy enough to go over your heaviest jackets, be comfortable over your bulkiest sweaters, and cover your lowest hemlines. (This, of course, excludes formal occasions, when you will need either an evening jacket or ankle-length coat.) The easiest fit comes with coats that have raglan sleeves or dropped shoulders. These styles give you the kind of shoulder and arm room you will need. Wearing a jacket when you try on coats will give you a good idea of how much room you will have. No sense feeling like a stuffed soldier in a brand new coat.

The second consideration is protection from the cold and from wet weather. Button-out linings are a good solution. The standard trenchcoat can work well for the day but the typical tan color doesn't translate well to the night. One way to solve this problem is to choose a trenchcoat in a dark color such as navy or black. This will look appropriate for day or evening. Whether in cotton or wool gabardine, a classic coat like this will work with most wardrobes!

Another type of coat that takes a lining is a "shell," an unlined coat with very simple lines that can take a fur lining, or even slip over a fur coat or a sweater-knit coat. The concept is the same as the trenchcoat, but the style of the shell is not quite as sporty.

There are some fabrics that are perfect for travel. Qiana®, for example, is featherweight and can fold to fit inside your handbag or briefcase. There are other nylons and blends that do similar tricks. These coats are excellent protection from the rain, and can save you concern about sudden showers whether you're dashing around town or traveling. With its shiny surface, this kind of coat can look dressy enough for evening and still be appropriate for work. An added bonus can be the reversible coat in this kind of fabric, an easy way to change the feeling of your coat to suit your spirit.

Fashion can be frivolous, but it also can be practical. The quilted down coat is a good example. Though army surplus stores have sold quilted coats for a long time, it is only recently that they have become such a part of the fashion scene. Although styles may change, quilted down does offer great protection from the cold and from wet weather. In addition, because the fabric takes color so well, it can be stunning night or day in everything from black to the boldest coloration.

Choosing a color for your coat may be a challenge depending on how varied your Capsules are. In general, it is wisest to pick the darkest color you have in your Capsules. A dark color is practical for many reasons including the ease with which it will work with your clothes, the fact that it will not show dirt or grease as much as a lighter color will, and that it will look as attractive during the evening as it will during the day.

THE TOTAL YOU

Before going further with your wardrobe, it may be worth a moment to analyze yourself, to look at your figure, your hair, and your makeup. To be truly comfortable in your clothes you must see the total you. You must know your own body and features and know what works best for you. Developing your own style is an essential part of a good working wardrobe. Though following fashion is certainly an interesting part of life, as kindred to the times as seeing the latest movie, hearing the newest music, or reading the current bestseller, all of these should reflect your own taste. But finding your own style takes time and testing.

Hair and makeup follow similar fashion trends. It is important to know not only what is the latest look but what is most flattering to you. Almost every major department store offers free sessions with beauty experts who will do everything from analyzing your skin to teaching you the latest cosmetic techniques. Stressing your needs to them, whether it is makeup for work, for evening, or for a special photographic session, will help them to help you.

While it is fun to try out exotic new looks in eye shadow, or daring new colors in lipstick, remember that makeup for work should look as natural as possible. That doesn't mean you shouldn't wear any; it does mean that whatever you wear should look fresh and light. There is a fascinating videotape from a cosmetics company which some stores show from time to time. In it, one of their women executives demonstrates how she creates her face every day in fourteen minutes. Although she uses a full range of cosmetics to cover every problem that a woman may have, from deep circles under the eyes to creeping smile lines, her finished look is attractive without being heavy.

Many cosmetic firms are now stressing skin treatment as much as makeup. Experts from these firms will analyze your skin to find out what type it is, what problems you may have and how best to deal with them. The treatment can include a full range of products, including everything from special soap to eye shadow, all geared to your skin's needs.

Like your makeup, your hairstyle should be flattering but not stiff or obvious. Hair that overshadows you is no more help than glaring makeup. Hair that gets in your way or causes you to brush it out of your eyes continuously can be disconcerting to you and to others. The simpler the hairstyle, the better it is for work. If you have long hair, try a style that takes it away from your face. That may be as easy as brushing it back and putting it into a plastic-coated rubber band, or may involve trying out new styles with barettes or combs.

A good haircut is very important, and like so many things that are good, it may cost more than you are accustomed to paying. But it, too, is an investment that can offer a good return. If your hair is well cut, you may find that you need fewer trips to the hairdresser and that you can take care of it yourself more easily. A really good beautician, like a good cosmetician, will assess your features and advise you on what will look best for you. No matter how much money you spend on your clothes, you will always look better if you pay attention to your total self. It is interesting that so many remarks about Nancy Reagan are about how well groomed she always is. Although her clothing is indeed expensive, it is the care and effort she puts into her total look that brings her compliments.

BUILDING ON THE CAPSULE CONCEPT

Once your basic Capsule is set, you may want to add to it. Your working wardrobe can contain a single Capsule with an infinite number of pieces based on a two color scheme, or it may be composed of different Capsules which interrelate. You might, for example, have one Capsule in black and white, and another in gray and yellow. These two groups may be combined within your working wardrobe since the four colors can all work together.

No one can blame you if you want more than two colors in your closet. But if you are adding Capsules, work around black or navy, not both. As you will see when we discuss accessories, this simplifies everything.

The Working Capsule charts offer suggestions for Capsule combinations. You may follow them exactly, make your own substitutions, or use them as a springboard for your own ideas.

Two of the suggested Capsules are geared to a tailored, suit look. These are the Black/Red and the Ivory/Tan. The other Capsules, the Navy/Wine, Forest/ Ginger, and the Gray/Brown offer a softer look. The Navy/Beige works around dresses. With all of them you can go from very dressy to almost casual, yet stay within the framework of an appropriate Working Wardrobe.

Remember, the emphasis is on quality; natural fibers and lightweight fabrics will hold their shape and last longer. At the same time, they are more easily adaptable to all climates. Investing in one Capsule is all you need for a Working Wardrobe. With it you can get at least forty different looks, enough for two months without repeating the same outfit twice.

REAL PEOPLE

The two women in this chapter have achieved success in their careers as well as in their wardrobes. They have learned to dress in a way that suggests their own personal style and good taste.

Each woman is in a different profession with different job demands and a different lifestyle. Yet there are certain common denominators: work that demands a good deal of travel, hours that go long past the usual five o'clock day, and high visibility. While each woman's taste and budget has grown with her position, each has had to develop her own working wardrobe. With this goal in mind, each has, whether consciously or not, used the Capsule Concept.

These women offer very different approaches to dressing—the tailored elegance of Hanne Merriman and the vibrancy of Kaaren Gray. While their styles are individual, they each offer ideas that may help you solidify your own working wardrobe.

Kaaren Gray

Kaaren Gray paints her wardrobe with splashes of color. For her, color is the essence of life. She surrounds herself with it and makes it her strongest statement. "To a great extent, the colors I want to wear are the colors I want to live with," says the tall, pale blonde editor of *House & Garden*. "Even now," after eleven years at *House & Garden* magazine she says "I get my ideas from everything in life. I may take a new look at the garden and see pretty flowers growing in combinations I never would have thought of. I could be influenced by seeing a woman on the street wearing something unusual, or even by looking at a plate of food that's been beautifully prepared and put together. It could be movies, theater, paintings, or anything around me that makes me rethink my colors. I cut out pictures, keep color books, and even write notes to myself on interesting color combinations."

Her clothing may sometimes bring a doubletake. Her Capsules are Purple/Red and Blue/Apricot and she works them back and forth. "I find it a lot of fun and very interesting to combine unusual colors. You can make something look a little better if you try the unusual. For example, take purple pants and put them with a turquoise blouse, and than add a red belt. You get a 'look' with it." She may invest in one special item that gives her the chance to play with color even more, a jacket, for instance, that can be used in many different ways. "One of the best investments I ever made," she said, "was a Mary McFadden jacket, in quilted silk with bright flowers on it. That has become the most fantastic thing. I can wear it with any solid silk dress. And then I can put together different combinations. For cocktail parties I have an apricot skirt. With it I wear a sleeveless silk blouse in a plum color, and belt in a very vivid blue. Other times I wear the same plum top with pants that are sky blue and my apricot cummerbund. So I'm having fun with it. And you could seriously wear it with a pair of jeans."

For this color expert, there is no such thing as "safe." It simply goes against her grain. "I'm sort of allergic to the idea of putting on a navy suit," she said. "I would wear the elements. I have a navy gabardine skirt that I wear a lot in the wintertime. But I would try to change it more for me, perhaps with a quilted jacket or combined with some other color rather than make it a fixed unit." Even when she has the basics, they have her special look. "I don't have a black suit," she went on, "but I do have a purple gabardine skirt and coat. It has the feeling of a suit but with a little more fashion. In fact, purple is my basic color." The other staple in her wardrobe is silk tunic blouses. She buys them in different colors to mix with pants or wear with skirts. She feels they give a little more "style" than T shirts or tailored tops.

The first time I met Kaaren, she wore a silk shirtdress in a brilliant royal blue. That shock of color stood out against her pale skin and flaxen hair. "Those silk shirtdresses are something I live in," she told me. And keeping to her offbeat style, she added, "I particularly like the ones that have an asymmetric neckline, or buttons off center. I find the look and the colors are sensational. And I can go right from work out to dinner."

As editor of a home furnishings magazine, Kaaren feels there's a certain responsibility to look good. But there's a lot of competition, too. "Just being in the Conde Nast building is like show and tell," she confides. That makes a stronger case for a sense of individuality. "It matters how you put things together," she told me, "whether it's just neatness or a certain style. You have to have your own point of view in the end." As for Kaaren, "my point of view is color."

Kaaren Gray: Working Capsule

Colors—Purple/Red. Blue/Apricot. Then throws in a wide range of bright accents.

Fabrics—Silks. Wool gabardine. Natural fibers.

Accessories—Shoes in brown or wicker. Bags can have accent textures, colors. Jewelry takes texture, like shells or beads, or has a chunky look.

Style—A colorful point of view.

Key words—Combinations. Color blocks. Unusual.

Hanne Merriman —————————————————————————————

She could barely speak English when she came to this country and now she's one of the few top women retailers in the U.S. She learned her English watching soap operas and her style watching other women. "You see it all the time in our store," says Hanne Merriman, the president of Garfinckel's. "New buyers come in, and within three months you can see a big change in the way they look." Ideas for dressing come fast and furiously—from designers, from the market, from people in the store. You can drown in a sea of ideas. "Everybody tries to become themselves very fast."

What does she look for when she's hiring? "If a young woman comes into my office for an interview, I don't think you can prejudge and say what she should be wearing. I like to see people in their own style of dressing. As long as she understands herself, her colors, and her style—that is what I would look for."

What colors appeal to this chic, blonde executive? "I'm comfortable in the beiges, browns and grays. Therefore, I tend to wear them." Keeping her wardrobe colors simple keeps her life simple too, a stark contrast to her work where every decision is complex. From what kinds of looks and what quantities to buy, to what stores to build and where to build them, she is kept constantly under pressure. "So when I get dressed," she said, "I want things to be easy. I don't want to spend a lot of time trying to think what I have to do. In the morning when I get up, I usually decide before my bath what I'm going to wear. Keeping my colors to beiges, browns, and grays means there are a lot of things that go together. When you start getting into lots of colors, you have to worry about your underwear, your hose, your shoes, your handbag." If she stays in the same kinds of colors, it's very easy. "It doesn't take you long to make decisions. The easier you make it, the better it is."

What she buys is usually separates, skirts, silk shirts, jackets, and sweaters. She adds on to the pieces she already has, updating her wardrobe with new shapes and textures. One Capsule she bought for a trip and now wears to work included a beige silk knit top and a soft dirndl skirt from Calvin Klein. She repeated the same pieces again in a deeper tobacco color. Then she added a string color cable knit sweater from Ralph Lauren, beige linen pants, and a macrame tunic top from Irka. Two other pieces were an ombre striped beige top and pants from Anne Klein.

All of these pieces worked together, so that every top could be worn with every bottom. To update this group the following year, she bought some purple accent pieces. "When the purples started coming out and I tried them on," she says, "it was another very comfortable color to dress with because it does tie in very much with the beiges. It just fit right in and it gives you a whole new feeling."

The important thing in dressing is not having to worry about your clothes and feeling comfortable. If fashion is a complicated business, it is Hanne's aim to make dressing with style as easy as possible.

 # Hanne Merriman: Working Capsule

Colors—Gray/Brown. Purple/Beige.

Fabrics—Gabardines. Tweeds. Silks. Linens. Stays with natural fibers.

Accessories—Watch. Two pairs of earrings for day: silver balls, gold balls. For evening: diamond studs. Gold bracelet. May wear gold chain with or without pendant. Keeps it down to a minimum.

Style—Clean and simple. Very neutral, very natural.

Key words—Comfort. Ease.

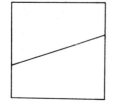

Chapter 2

THE ESSENTIAL ACCESSORIES

Fashion designers and fashion directors give as much thought and time to accessorizing clothes as they do to the clothes themselves. Taking one outfit, they can give it a dozen different looks.

Fashion shows are a good example of how this is done. Clothes may be repeated over and over, accessorized in totally different ways. Sometimes, even the professional eye can't tell that it's the same thing. In Paris and Milan, the European fashion capitals, or in New York, fashion shows are major productions, with music, models and choreography galore. Costs run in the tens of thousands of dollars and designers want their money's worth. Showing an outfit again and again, they make sure the press and buyers have seen it. A dramatic change can come in the colors or the style of the accessories, creating just enough difference to turn a buyer's head. How strange it is for buyers to go back to the showroom after seeing the clothes on the runway, and have trouble identifying the items they liked. What may look like a dumpy dress or a simple suit on the hanger, can look exotic and exciting when it's been sashed, bowed or bejeweled.

Some Seventh Avenue designers insist that their clothes be shown or advertised with only the accessories they select. Calvin Klein, Anne Klein, Halston, Bill Blass and Geoffrey Beene will all send their own belts, shoes, stockings, bags and jewelry if their clothing is being photographed. They know the difference the right accessories can make—and how the wrong ones can ruin an outfit.

The same thing can happen on a lesser scale too. I once did a fashion show of classic, simple clothing, well made but conservative. I treated each piece as if it were a jewel and polished each outfit with accessories. The show drew raves, because the merchandise looked exciting and wearable.

That's the trick used by fashion professionals when they're working on photography layouts. Every store, no matter what its price levels, wants its merchandise to look like a million dollars. That's the only way it will bring in mail orders. Whether an outfit costs $29.95 or $2,995 it has to look great. They may use unusual color combinations, or focus on a marvelous belt, a boldly colored scarf, an unusual necklace, a striking handbag. Suddenly a dull dress looks terrific. That's what makes the reader stop, look, and send in the coupon.

I was often surprised by the number of people who would order a total outfit by mail. Not just the skirt or the sweater. No, they would send in for those but also order the beret, the belt, and the bag as well. That's smart shopping. After all, it took a professional eye to put those pieces together in the way that looked fresh and best. Why not use that experience and taste level if you're not sure of your own.

Store windows are done with the same kind of care and attention to accessories. More time again is usually spent picking just the right accents than in pulling the clothes. The right shoe, the right bag, the belt, scarf and jewelry *can* make a difference. They can make something look like the latest thing or last year's discard. They can make it look expensive or cheap, dramatic or dull.

I always had fun doing a whole bank of windows, repeating one dress and accessorizing it differently in each window. For example, take a simple black wool shirtdress. Put a creamy turtleneck sweater under it, cinch it with a wide leather belt, use heavy textured stockings, low heeled walking shoes and a shoulder bag. You've got a great casual look. Take the same dress and fill in the neck with ropes of pearls and gold chains. Tie the waist with a thin black patent leather belt, use sheer tinted hose, patent leather slingback shoes, and a small black envelope bag. It's just right for going out to dinner. In between, this same dress can take a striped silk scarf worn as an ascot, or a simple gold chain and pendant. It can take leather pumps or patent slingbacks, bright colored accents or earthy toned ones. Each accessory changes the look of the dress and finishes it differently.

Accessories are as important to the Capsule Concept as the basic clothing elements. The Capsule Concept gives an easy formula for putting together a basic wardrobe. But every Capsule needs certain items to complete it. Creating a total look means that each clothing Capsule has its own set of essential accessories. Once this has been established, you can go beyond it to build on your Capsule. You will also be able to interchange accessories as well as clothes, going from one Capsule to another. Like the clothing Capsule, this is the foundation. Later on we'll go beyond the basics.

A man I know, a very successful lawyer, has won many cases on the Supreme Court, but can't put his clothes together. When his wife is at home, she coordinates his outfit, picking out the right shirt and tie to go with his suit, and even choosing his shoes and socks. When she is away on a business trip, she color codes his clothing so he can't make a mistake. That way if he decides on a brown suit, everything else he picks will be in the brown family too.

The Capsule Concept works the same way. By having a set of essential accessories for each Capsule, you can't go wrong. Some women always stay with these same accessories, keeping things to an easy decision. They find it makes for quick dressing all the time. Others enjoy collecting accessories, and use them for creativity in their clothes. But in both cases, they begin with the basics for their Capsule.

These essential accessories fall into five categories: shoes, handbags, jewelry, scarves and belts. Just as with your clothing, the essential accessories must be planned ahead. Shoes, for instance, are an expensive purchase and should be well thought out. My next door neighbor recently asked me what she should do with a pair of shoes she had just bought. "I don't know what's wrong with them," she complained, "but they don't seem to go with anything I own." Had she bought them with anything specific in mind? "Not really," she replied. Why did she buy them? "I just liked them," she said sadly. But shoes are too costly to be bought on impulse. They must be planned out like the rest of your Capsule. First, think about the clothes you have in your Capsule, what colors they are, and when you will be wearing them. Then set out with a specific color and style in mind. You may know that you need a pair of shoes for work, and that sometimes they will double to go out to dinner. You have just bought a navy suit and a wine shirtdress for your Capsule. Deciding on navy pumps or slingbacks in advance will save you from picking out bright green sandals because you lost your head.

A writer friend of mine recently sold some stories and celebrated with a shopping spree. She bought herself not one but two pairs of boots, each costing well over a hundred dollars. "Why boots?" I asked her, and she replied, "Why not? Aren't they in fashion?" Perhaps being too honest, I shook my head and said, "Not now." "What'll I do now?" she moaned. "Well, it doesn't really matter,"

I answered. "After all, you don't have to be concerned with the latest fashion."
"What do you mean?" she came back quickly. "I may not write about fashion,
but I certainly care about it. It's part of life." Now she is stuck with two pairs of
very expensive boots, because she bought them impulsively. She can't return
them because she wore them right away. She probably won't be wearing them
long though, because she hadn't thought out her purchase. In fact, just the
reverse. After we talked, and with careful planning, she started a Black/White
Capsule, and bought herself a beautiful black gabardine suit. "It cost more than
anything I ever bought," she told me, "but I never felt better about an
investment."

THE PROBLEM

Kathy B. had a wardrobe based on neutral colors, with a Capsule of beige and
gray. With her dark skin and dark hair, the light shades looked very attractive.
She stayed with simple, understated clothes, but wanted something to give
more depth to her dressing. She didn't like wearing scarves, and had a few
pieces of jewelry, namely a thin gold chain and some small inexpensive stud
earrings. She wanted to make more of a statement about herself.

THE SOLUTION

At 5 foot six, Kathy could carry clothes well, and needed accessories that were
in keeping. We decided to try earrings and necklaces that were chunky or large
in scale. For example, a set of oversized ivory beads looked wonderful with her
clothes. So did a very long rope of pearls that she could wind around four or
five times. She started wearing earrings that were much larger than the tiny
studs. She found large gold balls, and large silver balls that set off her face. She
also found a very wide ivory cuff bracelet and lots of thin silver bangles. Kathy
found that by wearing one jewelry item as a single statement, as for example,
the ivory beads one day, or all of the silver bangles the next, it gave her dressing
more punch. She also discovered that she loved looking for new jewelry in off
beat places.

Beige/Gray Working Capsule

		Colors			
		Beige	Gray	Accents	Will work with
A.	Jacket	Cardigan			All skirts and pants
B.	Jacket		Cardigan		All skirts and pants
C.	Skirt	Pleated			All jackets, blouses and sweater
D.	Skirt		Pleated		All jackets, blouses and sweater
E.	Pants	Trousers			All jackets, blouses and sweater
F.	Pants		Trousers		All jackets, blouses and sweaters
G.	Blouse	Shirt			All skirts and pants
H.	Blouse		Shirt		All skirts and pants
I.	Blouse				All skirts and pants
J.	Sweater	Pullover			All skirts and pants
K.	Sweater	Cardigan			All skirts and pants
L.	Dress	Shirtdress			All jackets on its own

Accessories

	Beige	Gray	Accents	Will work with
Earrings			Gold ball, Silver ball	Everything
Necklace			Ivory beads, Pearls	Everything
Bracelet			Ivory cuff, Silver bangles	Everything

THE PROBLEM

Judy B. had been working for several years as an agent for an insurance company. Her job required that she be in and out of her car, traveling around town to see clients. She liked to wear clothes that were tailored, often a blazer, shirt and skirt, but wanted to give them a more interesting look. She had a drawer full of scarves but didn't know what to do with them. She wasn't sure how to tie them, and felt they got in her way when she wore them. She liked jewelry but felt it didn't look right with her tailored clothes.

THE SOLUTION

After looking at Judy's scarves, we discovered that most of them were large squares in big floral patterns. She had acquired many of them as gifts and reflected the taste of others rather than of herself. Judy decided to invest in some oblong scarves, from very narrow to wide. With these she could dress up her shirts with a bow tie look, or fill in a neckline with an ascot, or wear them hacking style, or as a muffler inside or outside her jacket. She also bought two small squares to use as a handkerchief in a blazer pocket if she didn't want something around her neck.

As for jewelry, she decided to keep that simple, too. With her short hair and glasses, she didn't want a lot of interfering looks. She bought one pair of gold button earrings which she could wear every day. She also found an old gold bangle bracelet she hadn't worn in years which looked great with her clothes. By scaling down and keeping her accessories to a minimum, Judy retained her tailored look but gave it some style.

Black/Gray Working Capsule

		Colors		Will work with
	Black	**Gray**	**Accents**	**Will work with**
A. Jacket	Blazer			All skirts
B. Jacket		Blazer		All skirts
C. Skirt	Dirndl			All jackets, blouses and sweater
D. Skirt		Pleated		All jackets, blouses and sweater
E. Skirt		Tweed dirndl Black/Gray		All jackets, blouses and sweater
F. Skirt	Plaid Black/Gray/Red			All jackets, blouses and sweater
G. Blouse			White shirt	All skirts
H. Blouse			Ivory shirt	All skirts
I. Blouse			Yellow shirt	All skirts
J. Blouse			Red shirt	All skirts
K. Blouse		Shirt		All skirts
L. Sweater			Red pullover	All skirts

Accessories

Earrings			Gold button	Everything
Bracelet			Gold bangles	Everything
Scarves			Red square, Yellow square, Paisley oblong, Red oblong, Poulard oblong	Everything

SHOES

From a practical standpoint, you need at least two pairs of shoes in a Working Capsule. Feet need a change from one day to the next, especially if you're going to be doing much walking or standing. For a working Capsule like those in Chapter 1, you'll need a simple, tailored shoe. The shape most suited to this is a pump, and though it could have an ankle strap, a cross strap, a bow or some other detail, it should be a fairly simple, closed-heel, closed-toe shoe. Although styles may change, heels about an inch and a half to two inches are generally in good taste. It is the kind of shoe that can work with clothes for the office and can look attractive at a restaurant as well. A pump always works well with suits, tailored dresses, or even a skirt and blouse.

If you're buying a second pair, the next shoes could be slightly dressier, perhaps a slingback style, or ones with a closed heel and slightly open toe. (A good rule of thumb about open or bare shoes versus covered up ones is that if your clothing is covered up, your shoes should be, too.) Between the pump and the slingback, there will be enough flexibility to go from morning to evening. If you possibly can, find one manufacturer that makes shoes that fit your foot well and stay with it. No shoe is right, regardless of style, if it's not comfortable on your foot.

When trying on shoes, it's a good idea to bring with you at least one of the outfits from your Capsule. You may notice store display people carrying clothes around from one department to another, selecting shoes and accessories with the outfits in hand. They are the pros, and they don't take chances. There's no reason when you're spending your money, that you can't do the same thing. If you can, wear your clothes and try the shoes with them. Things look very different on the body than they do on the hanger or shelf. Colors change, too, and work differently when they are worn or mixed together. A shoe should generally be the same color or darker than your clothing. This gives a fluid line.

Bright or light shoes bring the eye downward. Wearing stockings that are a sheer tint of your skirt will help pull your look together too. Black or colored opaques or textured hose look best with heavy, textured clothing like tweedy skirts and thick knits. They usually need a low heeled shoe to give them balance. And for evening or during the summer, if you're wearing sandals, be sure to wear sandalfoot hose. That kind of attention to detail is one sign of a well-dressed woman.

HANDBAGS

A good handbag is an essential accessory for your daytime Capsule, of course. When a friend of mine broke her toe, I asked her how it happened. Embarrassed, she confessed she had dropped her handbag on her foot. Broken toes and aching backs are two good reasons not to stuff your life's possessions into your purse. It seems as if many women do. Not only is it uncomfortable, it looks sloppy, too. A handbag should hold the necessities; it should be a bag to hold in your hand, not a suitcase to weigh you down. If the necessities become overbearing, reevaluate them. Some women feel the need to carry a brush, comb, and cosmetics to work. A simple solution is to keep an extra set of cosmetics, perhaps even including a toothbrush and toothpaste at your office in a desk drawer. If your car is your office, consider the glove compartment as an alternative.

The color of your handbag should, of course, conform to your Capsule. Jane Tuman, fashion coordinator for Saks Fifth Avenue, remarked how often she is surprised at the number of well-dressed women who spoil their look with the wrong color bag. A burgundy bag can work with just about any color. If you prefer black, use it with your black Capsule. The same goes for navy and brown. But a black bag with a navy outfit looks misplaced and not well thought out.

Part of my job used to involve accessorizing the clothes for ads and catalogs. For one spring catalog we had sent dozens of bags ahead of time to the photographer's studio. That way we knew we would have lots to choose from. Oddly enough, as we chose a bag to go with the dress on the model being photographed, we found we kept reaching for the same bags over and over. Why? Because there were a few colors and shapes that were adaptable to all kinds of looks. A cream colored straw envelope popped up in picture after picture. It was an inexpensive purse, about fifteen dollars, but so flexible it went with just about everything. By the time we were finished with the session, everyone on the set, including the models, wanted that bag. We knew it would be a bestseller, and it was. That's the kind of accessory that's perfect for a Capsule because it adapts to a great variety of clothes.

Some women feel more comfortable carrying a shoulder bag, and if that's your preference, fine. One word of caution, however; there's nothing worse than being sideswiped by someone else's shoulder bag. If you do carry one, keep it small or hold on to it. This will also save you from getting pickpocketed as shoulder bags make easy targets. Even a small shoulder bag can fit inside a briefcase, if you need to carry both.

If your work requires that you carry a large amount of papers, a briefcase may be a necessity. The ideal purse will fit inside your briefcase, so that you look sleek and not like a bellboy trying to balance too many bags. (Some designers have even designed bags that go inside bags, rather like the Russian dolls you may remember from childhood.) But a small envelope or rectangular shaped purse should be able to slip inside most briefcases. Briefcases can offer the luxury of being used for more than just carrying papers. Some people use it as an overnight case. Others carry their lunch in it. Millicent Fenwick, the Congresswoman from New Jersey, showed me the bright red leather briefcase that she uses every day. "It's marvelous," she said, "because I can bring in homemade bread on one side and important papers on the other." And for some women, a briefcase is not a briefcase at all, but a colorful straw or canvas tote that holds everything they need.

Al Hackl, who is in the printing business, tells of a woman who came to work for his company more than ten years ago. She was the first woman in his industry to sell his product out in the field and her potential customers were all men. This very attractive woman wanted to look feminine but businesslike as well. She decided to carry a briefcase, but to make it look softer, she had it embroidered, and it worked well. She received many compliments on her briefcase and many sales in her orderbook.

Today it isn't necessary for a woman to use arts and crafts to be in the business world. Briefcases come in various sizes and colors and can be found in handbag departments as well as in traditional men's and luggage areas. There are some which look more feminine than others because of the color of the leather or the trim or the shape of the frame. It doesn't hurt to soften your look in this case.

SCARVES

Isadora Duncan overdid it, but two or three silk scarves can serve a multitude of purposes. An attractive scarf can add pizazz and change the look of a blouse, a suit, or a dress. The shapes may vary, but generally a medium sized square or oblong works best. These can be made into mufflers, ascots, bows, belts and ties. Naturally, the colors should complement what's in your Capsule, but this is also a good place to introduce new tones and accents too. For a Black/Red Capsule, you might have a purple scarf, a foulard print, and a boldly striped oblong. Or you might prefer strictly solids that you can mix together or wear alone. Or florals with lots of color.

Some women always wear a scarf with a coat. Leslie Stahl, the CBS news correspondent, wore a bright blue scarf with her dark coat on the evening news one winter. It not only brightened up her coat, but framed her face as well.

Just the way a scarf is tied too, can send out the message that you are fashion savvy. Some years the look is a bow to one side, other times it's a muffler worn just flipped over. Fashion magazines and store displays always show the latest look and it's easy to get the message.

Oblong scarves work well as mufflers, ascots, bows, and cummerbunds. The 54-inch bias scarf is the best size for a belt. The smaller 45-inch can be better at the neck. A small square can be used as an ascot or tied in a knot and worn under an open shirt collar. The very small squares that stores carry work as pocket handkerchiefs, a good way to perk up a jacket.

Old scarves should never be discarded if they're in good condition. About fifteen years ago I bought several silk foulard menswear squares in Bermuda. They're still in perfect shape, never go out of style with tweedy clothes, and I look forward to taking them out of the drawer each autumn. They're my personal signal that fall has begun.

The following illustrations show how you can tie your scarves to get the most mileage out of them.

The *bow* is made most easily with an *oblong scarf*. It can be made close to the neck or dropped lower, and can be worn inside an open neckline, over a jewel neckline, or under a collar. A pussycat bow can soften a suit or dress and change the look of an outfit to give your Capsule a feminine touch.

Illustration Courtesy Echo Scarfs.

The *hacking* style is another look made with an *oblong* scarf. It adds a sporty look to jackets and is great under coats. To make it, first fold the scarf in half lengthwise and place it around your neck so that you are holding the folded half in one hand and the two outside edges in the other. Then put both edges through the folded loop.

Illustration Courtesy Echo Scarfs.

A *tie* can be made easily with an *oblong scarf*. It can add a dash of color or pattern to a blouse, a sweater or a dress. Slip the scarf around your neck making the left side longer than the right. Then wrap the long end once around the short end and pull the long end through the top of the loop. You can adjust it to be high or low, to sit just under the collar like a man's tie or dropped lower for a softer look.

Illustration Courtesy Echo Scarfs.

The *pouf* is also made with an *oblong scarf*. To make it, first double the scarf around your neck, leaving one end longer than the other. Then loop the ends over each other, and pull the longer end through only part way.

Illustration Courtesy Echo Scarfs.

The *cowboy* style is made with a *square scarf* of any size, and can be done with anything from a small cotton bandana to a big silk floral. First fold the scarf into a triangle. Then place the point of the triangle in front and knot the ends in the back. This can give a great new look to a simple sweater or dress, and give another direction to your Capsule.

Illustration Courtesy Echo Scarfs.

The *jabot* is made with a *square scarf* and worn inside or outside collar of your blouse or dress. To make it, fold the square horizontally so that it becomes an oblong. Then flip the ends over one another.

Illustration Courtesy Echo Scarfs.

A *soft sash* around the waist is made with a *bias scarf*. It can be made into a cumberbund or finished with a bow. It can pull together a simple blouse and skirt or dress up a shirt and pants look. The bias scarf can also be made into a tie or bow and worn at the neck.

Illustration Courtesy Echo Scarfs.

BELTS

If scarves frame your face, then belts set off your waist and give a polished look to an outfit. They can complete a skirt and blouse to make it look like they're meant for each other. A good belt can replace an inexpensive sash that may come with a dress you buy. Basic belts should be one to two inches wide, of good quality leather, and though they may cost more than you like, they should last a very long time. Belts, like scarves, may go in and out of style, but they can remain a staple in your wardrobe. A good dark belt in a corresponding color to your Capsule, like black, brown, or navy, and one in wine, can be an excellent complement to your clothing Capsule. An interesting buckle can give the belt extra panache. One of the bestsellers in many stores is the expandable gold metal belt which works well with all kinds of looks from a.m. to p.m. Donna Karan, designer for Anne Klein & Co. suggests that a wine snakeskin belt is the perfect accessory for any outfit, whether dressy or sporty, daytime or evening.

JEWELRY

No matter what kind of work you do, whether it involves running an office or driving a carpool, a good watch is a necessity. It should run accurately, of course, and be of a simple design so that it works with all of your clothes. A leather or plain gold band is most adaptable to all looks. If you're fortunate enough to be able to afford a Rolex or something similar, enjoy it! While jeweled watches, ones with diamond trim, for example, are best left for evening, a dark leather band will take you through most of the day.

Some women feel naked without earrings. I know I do. But you don't need many pairs to give you that finished feeling. Two pairs—one in gold, and one in pearls, or a combination of pearls and gold—should give you flexibility for your Capsule. A button, ball, or shell design, or a simple twist or small hoop will go with your working wardrobe. These are the kinds of styles too, that will work well from morning to evening.

On a similar scale, open collars or plain necklines sometimes need a filler. Either a simple gold chain or pearls will usually do the trick. The chain can be very delicate, or if it is a heavier rope design, it can look great mixed with your pearls. Some women use pearls as their signature. Millicent Fenwick wears the same ones every day and evening. They're her. *Esquire* magazine once did an article on what distinguished "really rich" girls. The giveaways were cashmere sweaters and a single strand of pearls! Whether or not the pearls are real, the look is indeed rich. Another jewelry item that helps soften your look and adds dimension to your dressing is a bracelet. One classic design, like a bangle or link style, is all you need for the foundation.

THE BASIC ACCESSORY WARDROBE

What's been discussed so far are the very basics, the essential accessories. If you're just beginning a working wardrobe, or putting together a new Capsule, these are the essential accessories you'll need: two pairs of shoes, one handbag, one briefcase (if needed), two belts, three scarves, a watch, two pairs of earrings, two simple necklaces, and a bracelet. For your evening Capsule, include one pair of evening shoes and one evening bag. You may want to splurge on one smashing pair of evening earrings and one great necklace too.

But what about the extras, the excitement? When I designed sportswear for Herman Geist, some of my designs sold in the tens of thousands. But some of my favorite styles never sold well at all. This didn't seem to bother the owners of the firm, and one day I asked why. "Janet," one answered, "you design the icing on the cake. When buyers come to our showroom they ooh and aah. They think we have a very exciting collection. Then when they go home and write up their orders, they buy what is basic and what they know they can sell. They may buy just a few of your favorites because they won't sell as fast. But without them we would have a very dull line." In the same way, everyone needs the basics in their wardrobe. That's what we wear day in and day out. That's part of the Capsule Concept. Then comes the icing on the cake.

The following accessory charts are included to suggest how the essential accessories work with the Capsules detailed in Chapter 1. Like the clothing charts, they can be used exactly as shown, or modified to suit your needs and preferences.

Black/Red Capsule
Essential Accessories

	Black	Red	Accents
Shoes	Pumps, slingback		
Handbag	Envelope		
Briefcase		Portfolio	
Belts	Narrow		Gold expandable
Scarves*	Oblong	Square	Multi-stripe oblong
Watch			Gold
Earrings			Gold button, pearl button
Necklace			Gold chain, rope of pearls
Bracelet			Gold bangle

*See illustrations on ways to tie a scarf.

Brown/Gray Capsule
Essential Accessories

	Brown	Gray	Accents
Shoes	Pumps	Pumps	
Handbag	Shoulder bag		
Briefcase	Attache		
Belts	Narrow		Purple narrow
Scarves*	Oblong		Rust oblong, Purple oblong
Watch	Leather band		
Earrings			Gold ball, silver ball
Necklace			Gold chain, silver chain and pendant
Bracelet			Gold link

*See illustrations on ways to tie a scarf.

Navy/Wine Capsule
Essential Accessories

	Navy	Wine	Accents
Shoes	Pumps	Pumps	
Handbag		Envelope	
Briefcase		Portfolio	
Belts	Narrow	Wide	
Scarves*		Oblong	Navy/wine paisley print, mustard oblong
Watch	Leather band		
Earrings			Gold ball, pearl button with gold trim
Necklace			Gold chain, rope of pearls
Bracelet			Gold bangle

*See illustrations on ways to tie a scarf.

Ivory/Tan Capsule
Essential Accessories

	Ivory	Tan	Accents
Shoes		Pumps, Slingbacks	
Handbag		Clutch	
Briefcase		Attache	
Belts		Narrow	Brown narrow
Scarves*			Brown plaid square, ivory/brown/rust floral square, rust oblong
Watch		Leather band	
Earrings			Gold button, tortoise button
Necklace			Gold flat chain, Amber beads
Bracelet			Gold link

*See illustrations on ways to tie a scarf.

Forest/Ginger Capsule
Essential Accessories

	Forest	Ginger	Accents
Shoes	Pumps	Pumps	
Handbag		Envelope	
Briefcase		Tote	
Belts	Wide		Narrow
Scarves	Oblong	Oblong	Mustard square
Watch			Gold Band
Earrings			Gold buttons, Amber balls
Necklace			Gold chain, Amber beads
Bracelet			Gold bangle

Navy/Beige Capsule
Essential Accessories

	Navy	Beige	Accents
Shoes	Slingbacks, pumps		
Handbag	Clutch		
Briefcase			Rust envelope
Belts	Narrow		Rust narrow
Scarves	Paisley square, Floral square		Rust oblong
Watch	Leather band		
Earrings			Gold buttons, Pearl buttons
Necklace			Gold chain, Pearl rope
Bracelet			Gold link

REAL PEOPLE

Accessories can show artistry in your wardrobe. The two women profiled in this chapter take you from the essential elements that every woman needs to the fashion techniques that mark a woman with style.

Whether you enjoy wearing lots of accessories or would rather stay with the barest minimum, these women offer new ideas on how to dramatize and individualize your wardrobe.

Mona Shaker

Mona Shaker combines Middle Eastern mystique with Western practicality. She is a professor of English and the wife of a diplomat. Her nationality is Egyptian, but her style is international. With her jet black hair, olive skin, high cheekbones and flashing brown eyes, she exudes drama. "I feel clothing is art," she told me.

She talked about some of her wearable art. "I have one bolero that hangs on my walls. It's from old Russia, a wedding present from my mother. It's made of wine velvet embroidered with gold thread. Wearing this with her clothes, she makes it the focal point of an outfit. "I use it with a black silk or satin skirt and a very simple white blouse. The whole focus is that very interesting bolero."

Treating all of her jewelry as art as well, Mona is continuously creating new looks from the pieces she has. She gets her ideas from magazines or by looking at the real thing. But then she must have quite a collection of jewelry? "Not at all," she promises. I don't buy a lot, but I have a few basics that I play around with." For her, basics means pearls and gold chains. "Whether they're pearls or gold, I make them into chokers. I find that suits me. Then I hang a pin from the choker. This makes for a very dramatic look." Fortunate to have done a good deal of traveling, she has made it a point to pick up one or two pieces wherever she's been. Most of them are of semi-precious stones. Whether it's an old Turkish piece, or one that's an antique from India, she hangs it on a thin chain. "Gold chains are my basic element," she said. Along with her necklaces, Mona wears earrings, but makes sure these aren't too elaborate.

The other accent Mona uses is the scarf. With it she adds color, texture, and drama to her clothes. "I like shooting shades," she said, "like purples and lavenders. I don't go for pale tones. She uses those hot colors to brighten up her wardrobe. "Especially in the winter, when I have a lot of dark colors, and I want a note of life, I take a scarf in a brilliant color, a bold check or strong stripe, and that changes the whole look of the outfit." She has found that the very long oblong scarf is the size most adaptable to her needs. "With a great big bow at the neck or at the side, it dresses up a shirt and skirt and makes it special. I can go to a luncheon or a meeting and feel dressed up."

She also has fun with belts. Though she can't afford designer clothes, she can splurge on a St. Laurent sash or cummerbund. "You can compose a lot around belts," she told me. So she uses them to set off a bolero, or pull in a chemise, or frame a skirt.

Dressing in strong colors, with dramatic accents takes a little doing, and she's the first to admit it. "If I'm not comfortable in clothes I shrink in them," she confides, "as if I don't want to show." She shops carefully, trying things on several times before she buys, and always ready to turn them down if they aren't exactly right. "The most important thing I've learned," she says, "is knowing what looks good on me. I've trained myself to say no." But once she gets it home, she doesn't stop. Instead, she has dress rehearsals, trying on jewelry, scarves, belts, shoes and handbags, seeing what's best for a total outfit. "That way," she goes on, "I find it always looks better. I feel there is improvement for myself in every field," she says, "be it teaching, entertaining, meeting people or dressing. There is always something new to learn."

 # Mona Shaker: Working Capsule

Colors—Beige/Black. Red/Navy.

Fabrics—Silks. Linens. Egyptian cottons.

Accessories—One of a kind. Semi-precious stones. Chokers. Chains. Centerpieces. Small earrings. Rings on one finger. Boleros. Cummerbunds. Scarves in long oblongs to be tied, sashed or bowed.

Style—Clothing as art. International.

Key words—Drama. Color. Details.

Dot Roberts

Small, slim, gray-haired, and perennially tanned, Dot Roberts is an energetic woman who keeps herself and her business in great shape. She goes mountain climbing for pleasure, but she climbed a bigger mountain when her husband died just a few years ago. She was really shaken when her partner in business and marriage passed away. "The most important thing in life is the ability to change," she told me. So instead of letting herself and the business slip, as the president of Echo Scarfs, she set out to make her company bigger and better.

With a consuming business and a life filled with constant travel, Dot's got to be well-organized. Her approach to dressing shows it. She wears mostly suits, "I'm a good suit person. And it works well because I travel so much." She changes their look with different blouses, which become her mainstay. "I think silk blouses are the most useful thing in your wardrobe," she told me. "You can wear them all year long, they go with.everything, and they always look right."

But for Dot, it's the accessories that make the difference. "I don't change my clothes around because of the time element," she says. "I never decide the night before what I'm going to wear. But when I get up in the morning, I have to get the scarf, the pantyhose, the shoes and the bag." To make it all work better and faster, she has organized her clothing by color. While some people never get beyond sorting their clothing into clean and dirty, Dot has everything arranged in groups. "I have my whole closet by color and style," she explains, "with blouses on one side and skirts and jackets on the other, and everything going in tones. They hang in the beiges, the browns, the grays, and black."

Naturally, she's got her accessories organized too. She keeps her shoes and handbags all lined up by color. But it's her pantyhose that used to be the biggest headache. "I have a lot of pantyhose, and now I have them by color, too. I have black, brown, gray, taupe, and wine, and then I've separated them into sheer and opaque. That way I don't waste any time." It's with her scarves that she makes her fashion point. "And I can add color, pattern, or a new fashion look with them too." Just back from a four day trip to Canada, she said, "I didn't take much with me, but I was able to keep changing the look of my clothes. Some of the people I was with were always the same, but we were meeting new people all the time at lunches and dinners, and I had to get different looks. I brought two basic outfits of a skirt and jacket, in black and beige, a couple of blouses and sweaters, two pairs of shoes, one bag for day and one for evening, and eight scarves. With those scarves I could do everything from a cowboy look to an ascot, from a bow to a pocket handkerchief. I worked the clothes back and forth, and used my scarves as accents to create the fashion."

She may be in Canada, Paris, Milan, Hong Kong, Tokyo, or the U.S., and she gets her inspirations everywhere. "I love to look at people," she said. "That's how you get new ideas and learn what looks best on you.

With clothes being such an investment, people should plan their wardrobe carefully, and buy things that can go from season to season." Says this clear headed dynamo, "The most important thing is to get your clothes organized and know your own style. Then you can get on with the business of life."

Dot Roberts: Working Capsule

Colors—Black/Gray, Beige/Brown.

Fabrics—Wools in gabardine or tweed, Silks.

Accessories—Always a scarf. Pin. Bracelet. Watch.

Style—Suited to a T. Silk shirts galore. A Tweedy Lady.

Key words—Crisp. Clear. Comfortable.

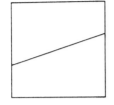

Chapter 3

THE IMAGE OF SUCCESS

For the businesswoman in the '80s, there may well be a move toward a working uniform. The suit, for the corporate world, is the quickest signal of executive status. How does the management male distinguish the female secretary from the female executive? Clothing is the easiest way to tell them apart. Dressing in the corporate uniform identifies the woman manager as one of their own. But, in no way must she mimic a man. The stereotype of the Girl in the Gray Flannel Suit is an insult to women. A woman can look competent and professional without sacrificing her femininity.

Trisha Parson is an executive recruiter who often advises her clients to slip on their uniform. But she stresses the importance of also looking feminine. For her the suit distinguishes the woman with a job from the career woman. The stress on woman comes with jewelry, hair, and makeup done just right.

WHAT YOUR CLOTHING SAYS ABOUT YOU

Clothing acts as a cue for those around us. It helps strangers identify us, and reinforces the image held by acquaintances and friends. It's what people see first and remember. Knowing how to use clothing to establish yourself in whatever role you want to play can help win that role more quickly.

There are many women who are not sure of what role they want to play. There are others who intentionally wear the wrong costume, and send out the wrong message, afraid that dressing well might detract from their intellectual profile. One male senior partner in a law firm told me about a young woman who had entered the firm with high marks from law school and a brilliant future ahead of her. The only problem was that no one in the firm wanted to introduce her to clients. "We were desperate," he said. "We wanted to keep her but she dressed so badly. We couldn't let any of our clients meet her." Fortunately for this young woman, some very good friends took her aside and taught her the rules of dress. Her appearance improved markedly, and says the senior partner, "she's now on her way to becoming a partner herself."

If the suit is the symbol of the corporate woman, for other women in other fields, there are other such signals. In retailing, the hierarchy is established not only by the price of one's clothes, but by the "forwardness" of their design. While young assistants may wear clothes by Liz Claiborne and Jones, the buyers they work for dress in Calvin Klein. The upper management women may show their fashion savvy by wearing such Italian designer clothes as Missoni or Armani. And the top echelon executives will buy the French fashion establishment—Yves St. Laurent, Chloe, and Dior.

Women in public life face an even greater problem. Their image can become a target for public scorn or envy. Certainly they do not wish to be under constant attack by the press—or perhaps even worse, totally ignored. They must have a total understanding of what suits them best, plus an eye for detail, if they are to maintain that unmistakable aura of self-confidence and public presence.

Our clothing immediately establishes us in some sort of social order, whether or not we are aware of it. The bright business school graduate who went to interview for a banking position was told that her record was excellent but she obviously did not want a job in that field. Shocked, she went home and looked at herself in the mirror. Only then did she realize the kind of message she was sending out. She had dressed for the interview in the type of outfit she often wore, a full printed dirndl skirt and a soft peasant blouse. The stranger from the bank had suggested she might be more at home in journalism or the arts. In fact, she hadn't really wanted a job in banking and now holds a very responsible position with a graphic arts firm in Texas. She had revealed herself through her clothes without even knowing how much she was telling about herself.

If you know what role you want to play, you can use clothing to get the part. The secretary who wants to be an executive will get there faster if she starts dressing like the women above her rather than those around her. The upper echelon will identify her as one of their own (provided, of course, that she's capable of the work). The woman who wants to be the chairman will have a better chance of getting the position if she looks like a leader. The woman who wants to establish herself as financially well-off can send out signals that say she is used to wealth.

When Linda Silverman made a conscious decision to climb the corporate ladder, she resolved never again to wear pants to work. "When you're trying to get up the corporate ladder," she told me, "there's a point when everybody has the same background. When you want to be recognized, a lot is the way you project yourself. You have to play the part before you get it."

Until that time she had dressed casually in her job as a secretary at Sotheby's, often wearing a pair of corduroy pants and a shirt or sweater. That was typical dressing for many of the secretaries and assistants at the Madison Avenue auction house. "I looked at the other women around me and at the one woman who was on top. I realized she never wore pants. You could really get a feeling of who held what job by what they wore."

So she put aside the corduroy pants and jeans, and started buying clothes that looked and felt expensive. Wearing well-made jackets and skirts in fine wools and blouses and dresses in elegant silks immediately established her as a cut above the crowd. It also indicated her appreciation of good things. Now, as head of Sotheby's contemporary department, she finds her seasonless clothes move easily not just from one climate to another, but look great during the day as well as for dinners, openings, and receptions.

With a Capsule based on blues and greens, she chooses clothing that is soft rather than hard tailored, and prefers a look that is conservative. Speaking about her image, she says, "I think you represent yourself as well as your firm. I can't go around talking about millions of dollars worth of paintings if I don't have a look that says quality, and at the same time, is always feminine."

Clothing can signify class status, political identification, profession and rank. As Barbara Dickstein, museum specialist and collector of twentieth century clothing for the Smithsonian Institution told me, "Clothing, more than anything else—more than furniture, more than jewelry—clothing represents a person. No matter what the time frame, she went on, "clothing is always a symbol of who you are. It tells your status, your role in life, your social position." The sign of nobility in seventeenth-century France was the use of velvet. Peasants and others of the lower class were not permitted to wear it. A century before, in Germany, during a peasant uprising, one of the demands was to be allowed to wear the color red, until then permissible only for the upper classes. Royal blue and purple were the colors of the court throughout much of Europe. Only the nobility could be seen in them.

In China, the blue cotton pant suit became the symbol of the revolution. But as Nancy Kissinger told me when she was there, "The women were just dying for some pretty clothes, a pretty blouse or earrings." And in fact, more and more of them are now wearing more colorful and more feminine clothes.

Like many women, the wife of the former Secretary of State was often tempted to adapt local customs to her way of dress. But on one trip it backfired. "I was going out one night in China, in slacks, and Henry was very upset." Why? "You are an American," Dr. Kissinger told his wife. "If you were home, you would dress for an official dinner in a long skirt or something like that. You wouldn't go around in pants." But defending herself, Nancy insisted that she might indeed wear velvet slacks. But the man who broke new ground with the Chinese persisted. "You are representing the female portion of the United States," he said. "You should look like a westerner." And then he drew a strange picture. "How would it look," he asked, "if I suddenly went out in a pyjama suit? You'd think I'd gone crazy." And it was that image that made her realize how important the symbolism of dressing is. And in fact, in her travels around the world, she wears clothing made only by American designers as a way of signaling her belief in the creativity of the American fashion industry.

THREE DECADES OF FASHION

If the distinctions in clothing and class are less obvious today, the symbols are still there. The subtle differences are needed to send messages of social alignment. The significance of what we wear can be seen easily if we go back and trace the major trends of the last thirty years. In each decade there were clear signals being sent out about what was happening in society in general and for women in particular.

The 1950s represented for many a return to normalcy. For the first time in a decade, husbands and wives were home together, raising 3.2 children, buying a home in suburbia, and facing the happy prospect of prosperity. The role model was the Man in the Gray Flannel Suit. For the mainstream of America, the bulk of the middle class, success in the business world was a vitally important message to be sent out. Certain items of clothing became the acknowledged mark of that success. For women, the status symbol was the good leather handbag. The woman who could afford an alligator pocketbook and shoes was the walking symbol of her husband's achievements. Other luxury items took on this importance, namely the cashmere sweater, especially one with a mink collar. After the years of deprivation brought about by World War II, luxury items were a sure sign of social and financial success. The man who could buy his wife a mink stole had obviously "made it". And the woman who had all of these trappings, the alligator bag, the fine leather shoes, the cashmere sweaters and the mink wraps was the woman who had done well in life.

This same period also witnessed the birth of a new female identity, the "career" woman. Many women had begun working during the war years and found that they liked it. They enjoyed their financial independence and their personal sense of identification. For these women, sportswear became a new symbol of freedom. Here was an opportunity to put together a number of looks. For the first time, clothes did not have to be worn in one and only one way. Said Barbara Dickstein, "People like Evan Picone started making skirts that weren't part of suits, finishing them with little notched details that became their signature. Jeanne Campbell designed separates for Sportwhirl, and Tina Lesser and B.H. Wragge were big names." Women who wore these clothes were signaling that they wanted to be free from the past and its restrictive nature of dressing. Fashion was acknowledging this attitude and providing a means of expression.

In the 1960s clothing took a whole other turn. The beginning of the decade was marked by fireworks of color from a suddenly social Italian nobleman by the name of Emilio Pucci. His dazzling prints in swirls of shocking pinks, deep turquoises, and passionate purples sent women from every social strata scurrying to buy their signature Puccis. The count could never have signed so many dresses, but they were worn by just about every woman who wanted to show her fashion savvy and social status. Obviously, those who could afford a real Pucci were part of the "upper class", and for the rest, the better the copy, the higher one's social rank.

But as the war in Vietnam took on more importance, it became necessary to show not wealth but rather political leanings. "Clearly, clothing was never more important than in the Sixties when it was used as part of the revolution," said Mrs. Dickstein. "You identified yourself and who you belonged to by the way you dressed. The uniform of the war was tie-dyes and jeans. There was no question what side you were on," she explained. For the liberals, tie-dyes and jeans were their signal of sympathy, not only to the anti-war effort but also to "the cause" whether it was mistreated Indians or underpaid grape pickers. But if so many people wore jeans, how could one identify the patrons from the poor, the art collectors from the grape pickers? A distinction needed to be made. It came in the form of status initials. Everyone could afford Levis, but only a few could buy shoes from Gucci. Fewer still could afford handbags made by Louis Vuitton. The upper crust liberal became easy to recognize. Her uniform was a T-shirt, jeans, and a blazer—with Gucci shoes and a Louis Vuitton bag. She might even throw a Gucci scarf around her neck. After all, a plain T-shirt left one feeling a little bare.

Under the T-shirt lay the next stage of clothing symbols. To bra or not to bra became the dilemma of women in the Sixties. Women's liberation could take many forms, but none was so clear as the symbolism of this piece of clothing. Bra burning became a major event around the country, and from coast to coast women bounced about eager to show their alliance with the women's movement. For some that was as far as their commitment to liberation went. But for all it was a significant way of saying that they would no longer be bound by the old rules.

While the bras were burning, the status initials were losing their exclusivity. It had come to a point where cheap copies were being hawked by sidewalk vendors on every street corner. Something new was needed. In the early Seventies the designers arrived. Suddenly, big stores started opening designer shops, carrying Calvin Klein and Anne Klein, and others smart enough to make sportswear that was attractive, expensive and identifiable. Bill Blass and Geoffrey Beene got the message too, and opened new divisions called respectively, Blassport and Beene Bag. It was similar to the French going from couture to ready-to-wear. American designers went from dressing the ladies who lunch to clothing the career woman. A whole new vehicle for status symbols arrived. The women who had been liberated in the Sixties now turned their eyes on a successful career in the Seventies. They could signal their success by wearing designer clothes. Those who had made it could afford to spend big sums on their working wardrobes.

The Seventies ended with the mushrooming of designer merchandise. No longer did the labels appear only on expensive clothing. They could be on one's fragrance. Or one's cosmetics. Or one's bed linens. Or on one's behind. The last signature of a designer became the one on the back of a pair of jeans. So much for the cult of the designer. But what next?

Many people see jewelry as the next status symbol. Barbara Dickstein pointed out a recent cartoon showing a mother observing her daughter in a T shirt and jeans. "Darling," asks the mother, "don't you think you should wear some gold jewelry so people don't get the wrong idea?". The Fashion magazines have been doing feature spreads on up and coming jewelry designers. Their time may be now. One woman, Elsa Peretti, has already become established as one of the most important people in twentieth century jewelry, working in the medium of silver, with a very contemporary flair. Belts by Barry Kieselstein-Cord, made with buckles of sculptured silver or bronze, are already an important status symbol. Paloma Picasso, daughter of this century's famous artist, is designing jewelry for Tiffany's.

THE PROBLEM

Anne P. had grown up in a small southern town where most of the women wore dresses. Her wardrobe was similar, and she enjoyed wearing dresses to work. When her firm promoted her and sent her to their main office in New York, she found herself in a very different atmosphere. The women who worked with her dressed in much more tailored clothes, and they eyed her with a certain amount of distrust. In order to establish her own credibility and authority, she found that she had to change her way of dressing.

THE SOLUTION

Most of the dresses Anne had worn in the south were in floral prints and often in pastel colors. We found she had a much stronger look when wearing darker colors, and we could still keep her Capsule to dresses as she preferred. Working around navy and tan, she selected variations of the shirtdress. To start, Anne bought three dresses, a navy silk, a tan and white striped silk, and a navy and tan geometric print. She already had a navy cardigan jacket that could go over any of these dresses as well as one or two she had from the south. Later on she added a navy and white checked dress. With all of these she could also wear a tan jacket which came with the new dress. Anne still could feel comfortable in her dresses, but she established an air of authority and assertiveness. Her investment in dressing came to $320.

Navy/Tan Dress Capsule

	Colors			
	Navy	Tan	Accents	Will work with
A. Jacket	Cardigan			All dresses
B. Jacket		Cardgan		All dresses
C. Dress		Shirtdress		Both jackets or on its own
D. Dress		Striped shirtdress Tan/White		Both jackets or on its own
E. Dress	Small print Shirtdress Navy/Tan			Both jackets or on its own
F. Dress	Checked shirtdress Navy/White			Both jackets oron its own

Accessories

Shoes	Pumps, Slingbacks			Everything
Handbag		Envelope		Everything

THE PROBLEM

Carolyn G. was a teacher who had spoken out at several school board meetings, and had become involved in local political issues. After two years, she found herself being promoted as a candidate for the state assembly. The idea appealed to her and she decided to actively campaign. But her classroom clothes were more appropriate for the after-school program than for after-dinner speeches. She had very little money to spend, but needed clothes that would upgrade her image. Her opponent, a very rich businessman, had an attractive wife whose good looks and pretty clothes often drew the cameras. Somehow Carolyn had to get the focus of attention on herself but still remain a serious candidate.

THE SOLUTION

Carolyn was most comfortable in skirts and jackets. We worked out a small Capsule based on navy and red. She bought two suits, one in navy, the other in red. Either jacket could go with either skirt. Then she selected three blouses, one navy, and the other two in white. But what made her wardrobe come to life were the four silk scarves she bought, each in a very bright color. She chose red, yellow, green and purple, and wore a different one each time she went out campaigning. The hot colors worn at her neck, caught the attention of her audience, and at the same time, her jacket and skirt gave her the serious, sincere image she wanted.

Navy/Red Image Capsule

	Colors			Will work with
	Navy	**Red**	**Accents**	**Will work with**
A. Jacket	Blazer			Both skirts
B. Jacket		Blazer		Both skirts
C. Skirt	Pleated			Both jackets will make suit with Navy jacket
D. Dress		Pleated		Both jackets will make suit with Red jacket
E. Blouse	Shirt			Both skirts
F. Dress		Shirt		Both skirts
G. Blouse		Shirt		Both skirts

Accessories

	Navy	Red	Accents	Will work with
Shoes	Pumps			Everything
Handbag	Shoulder bag			Everything
Scarves			Red oblong, Yellow oblong, Green oblong, Purple oblong	Everything

THE CAPSULE APPROACH TO SUCCESSFUL DRESSING

Women need not resign themselves to the idea of bland uniform dressing. With not only jewelry, but scarves, belts, handbags and shoes, a suit or dress can take on different looks and moods. No woman should lose her femininity. To quote from investment banker, Mary DiGiacomo, "Femininity is my greatest asset."

To look feminine and successful you must be aware of how you put yourself together. The Capsule Concept can help enormously because it creates an organized wardrobe for you. With quality clothing and accessories, you don't need a lot of items in your closet to look successful. Using just two colors and pieces that interrelate, dressing can be almost effortless yet bring you lots of compliments. With the Capsule approach you will be dressing in a professional manner and sending out a signal of self-assurance.

To see just how strong your signal is, take the Image Quiz on the following page.

Image Profile

		Yes	No
1.	Do you consider yourself a success?		
2.	Do you want to stay at your present job level?		
3.	When you are getting dressed, do you think about how you want to be perceived?		
4.	Do you dress like other women at your job level?		
5.	Do you dress like women at a superior job level?		
6.	Do you feel you look as successful as you are?		
7.	Do others perceive you to be at a higher level than you are?		
8.	Are there other women at work whose style of dressing you admire?		
9.	Do you often receive compliments on the way you look?		
10.	Do you feel comfortable in your clothes?		
11.	Do you feel well put together in your clothes?		
12.	Do you look at other women for fashion ideas?		
13.	Do you read fashion magazines regularly?		

		Yes	No
14.	Do You feel feminine in your clothes?		
15.	Do you look feminine in your clothes?		
16.	Do you wear real jewelry?		
17.	Are your shoes real leather?		
18.	Are your handbags/briefcase real leather?		
19.	Are your clothes made of natural fibers?		
20.	Do you buy the best clothing you can afford?		
	Total		

Score two points for every "yes" answer. Deduct two points if you answered "yes" to Questions 2 and 4.

- If you scored 36 points, you have a great image. Congratulations!

- If you scored 28–34 points, you're almost there.

- If you scored 22–26 points, keep working at it.

- If you scored below 22 points, you need more help. Read this chapter again!

REAL PEOPLE

As their careers climb, most women find a need to change their image, upgrading it to meet that of their new peers. The women in this chapter discuss how they have developed their image. For them it has been a particularly difficult problem. They are women in the public eye.

Both of these women know how important it is to project the right image, and have taken the time to study themselves and learn what kinds of clothing suit them best. In this chapter each of them talks about what goes into achieving a successful image, one that pleases them and the public too.

Nancy Reagan

Nancy Reagan may have played the role of the girl next door in the movies, but she's always made sure that that isn't really her image. You never would have seen her running next door in her bathrobe to borrow a cup of sugar. "Even then," she told me, her eyes opening wide, "they didn't want you to come out with curlers in your hair." Not that she would have anyway. As the debutante daughter of an Illinois doctor, and as a drama student at Smith, she lived in an aura of money and class. And if one were to suggest that her style came from the direction of the movie moguls at MGM, she takes offense. "You're the one who sets the tone for yourself," she says, "nobody else does."

With her contained manner, regal bearing, size six figure, high cheekbones and large wide-set eyes, she fits right into the role of First Lady. The day we talked she wore a gray and brown paisley blouse, a gray wool dirndl skirt, simple gold button earrings, a gold link bracelet on each arm, and a gold necklace. Her hair, softly streaked in shades of honey and gold, was perfectly in place. Her makeup was faint, with just a touch of lipstick. Her overall look was understated, well groomed, and all in good taste.

She feels that any woman can develop good taste and a distinctive style. "That's just exposure," she told me. But what about the woman who isn't surrounded by Beverly Hills luxury or Madison Avenue chic? "Any woman sees magazines and goes to movies," she maintained, and those are just two ways to be observant. Like all women of style, Nancy Reagan keeps her eyes alert for what is new, what is attractive, and what is happening in the fashion world. Then she adapts it to her own personal look.

What sort of advice does the First Lady have for the woman who is just starting out or having trouble finding her own look? With great conviction she states, "Get a three-way mirror and look at yourself from all sides." As for accessories, "if in doubt whether it's too much, take it off," she says. For the woman who tends to follow every fashion trend, no matter what it may be, she adds, "I would tell her not to follow fads. I think that people who are slaves to fashion or the latest fashion gimmick make a big mistake." With an edge of indignation in her voice, she goes on, "During the miniskirt phase, in the 1960s, it used to kill me to see older women in miniskirts. It just looked ridiculous." With the confidence that comes from success, she says, "There's a certain charm and beauty to any age if you dress that age."

One would assume that style comes easily to a woman who has seemingly endless amounts of clothing. But Nancy Reagan suggests that she feels less is better. "I don't like a lot of frills and fusses," she told me. "Anything that's simple works for me."

If Nancy Reagan always looks well groomed, she claims it's because she keeps things nice and simple. "I'm really basically a soap-and-water girl. I don't wear a lot of makeup." In the days when she traveled a lot, campaigning for her husband, she found that it helped to keep things pared down. "Everything's a problem for you during the campaign, because there's not enough time. You were lucky if you could get back to wash your face," she says shaking her head. For her the solution lay in a working wardrobe of knits. "The knit suits were so marvelous," she exclaimed, "because they didn't wrinkle. I never had to bother with them. I could put them on early in the morning and go all day and night."

When Nancy Reagan adds to her wardrobe, it's always with a thought to the clothes hanging in her closet. "I am not one who throws everything out at the beginning of a season and starts all over again. And," she adds, "I don't think anyone can afford to." Her wardrobe is a mix of old and new. "I hang onto things a long time." she revealed. "I have my second inaugural gown in Sacramento, and that goes back a long way. In fact," she continued, "I might still even have my first one if they hadn't torn it off my back."

How does she manage to update outfits that may go back five or six years? "I mix my clothes around," she says proudly. "I'll mix an Adolfo skirt with another blouse or jacket, switch things around with different outfits." Is there a point when the old favorites no longer look right even when they're mixed with the new? "That's when you get rid of them," she says adamantly.

Although Nancy Reagan has always enjoyed clothes, like many women she confesses, "I'm not crazy about shopping. I like clothes but I can't do what a lot of my friends do, shop all day and stand all day for fittings. That would be very boring." Her approach to shopping reflects her general attitude. "I know what I want pretty quickly, and I don't want to waste a lot of time."

Whatever she purchases for herself, Nancy Reagan makes sure that it fits her own image. As to the notion of other women adopting her look because it's the rage, she laughs and says, "I'd be flattered. But I think you have to find your own particular style, what's good for you, and go with that."

Nancy Reagan: Image Capsule

Colors—Red is her favorite, day or night. Also likes black and white for evening.

Fabrics—Wools, silks. Lots of knits.

Accessories—Always simple: earrings, bracelet, necklace.

Style—Understated. Classic clothes. Distinctly feminine.

Key words—Elegant. Tasteful.

Maureen Kindel ───────────────────────────────────

Maureen Kindel sends out a strong message in her picture at City Hall. "I am the first woman in the history of Los Angeles to hold this job," she told me. So the President of the Board of Public Works had her photograph taken wearing a hard hat. It isn't an image that most people like, particularly the men who work with her. She is also on the boards of civic organizations and private foundations from California to New York and Washington, D.C. For her, the trappings of achievement are as important as the accomplishments themselves because they relay her status to the rest of society.

What are the trappings? "Wearing good jewelry," she says "is terribly important." For her jewelry is an investment in her own future. "I think in terms of power, that's where a woman should spend her money. Because jewelry is a symbol of money, and money is a symbol of success and achievement." Given the choice between an expensive designer suit and a piece of good jewelry, she would opt for the latter. "Find a good facsimile of the suit," she suggests, "and use the remaining money on a tiger's eye or other semi-precious necklace." She also believes in buying good handbags, because "you can put it right out in front of somebody," like a quick flash of success.

She sees fur as an excellent signaling tool, "It is extremely important for me to dress on the same level as the wives of the other board members." That, to me, is how one translates power," says Maureen. "Achievement and power are what our society looks up to." Even if the mink coat takes a good bite of her income, she feels it is justified. "It is a matter of priorities. Women must put it on their back because that promotes them. They should not feel guilty about that." In fact, she says, because of the power of that message, "I think a mink coat is a terrific buy." If you can't afford mink, pick a less expensive fur, she suggests, but definitely pick a fur. At the same time, she is careful to wear her coat only when it is appropriate. Out in the field she is more likely to wear a raincoat, and only she knows that it is lined with fur.

This hard hat commissioner takes her femininity very seriously. She dresses in soft, rather than strictly tailored clothes, never wears pants, and loves luxurious fabrics. "I want to remind people that I am feminine, continually, by my dress, my demeanor, and by my actions," she says. If she is a woman with strong convictions, she has found that this comes through loud and clear to others. "When I am in a group of women, I've been told many times that I come on too strong. It is a negative, this strength that I project." By dressing softly she feels she can tone down that image. "I have to use clothes to reinforce my feminine side."

How does she dress to look soft but self-assured? If she wears suits, which she does "because they are convenient," she says she would "always wear a very feminine blouse and very good jewelry." Her favorite designers are not the well-known, high-priced ones. "I have a prejudice against very expensive clothes," she concedes. The day we talked she wore a black and white polka dot pleated skirt and blouse with a red cardigan sweater. This sweater look is one she has come to enjoy even more than the typical suit jacket or blazer. "This is the perfect kind of outfit," she says. "I can wear the blouse with other things, and when I wear it with this skirt it looks like a dress." Her other favorite outfit is a "Calvin Klein black skirt, candlelight blouse, and black sweater. It's a wonderful look. I think that a lot of women will find out what a great pleasure sweaters are to wear," she says, obviously enjoying the softness in both look and feel.

Maureen Kindel has obviously given a great deal of thought to the signals she sends out. "There is a way to look elegant, classy, and powerful," she states. "I am really tired of seeing women in gray flannel uniforms." Though she is the first woman to hold her job, she wants no one to think of her in masculine terms. "I feel feminine, I am feminine, and I want to be feminine in the most positive way."

 Maureen Kindel: Image Capsule

Colors—Black/White with accents of Red

Fabrics—The luxury touch: Silk, Cashmere, Fur.

Accessories—Only the best. Precious or semi-precious stones. Expensive bags and expensive shoes.

Style—Knows where she's going and what she wants. Uses her clothes to soften her image, strengthen her success.

Key words—Determined. Successful. Feminine.

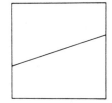

Chapter 4

THE EVENING CAPSULE

If daytime clothes are for the serious side of life, evening clothes are for fantasy and fun. A sensational evening outfit can be a great lift after a hard day at work, a chance for frivolity after the restrictions of more tailored clothes. But your evening clothes can also be well organized so that again you can have flexibility in your wardrobe. The Capsule Concept can be easily extended into the evening.

THE EVENING LOOK WITH SEPARATES

With just five pieces you can create many looks. A dressy jacket, a skirt, a pair of pants and two dressy tops can be the basis of a successful evening Capsule. Naturally, these pieces should be worked around two compatible colors—for example, one capsule could be composed of burgundy and winter white.

The focal point for after five can be an evening jacket. As an essential part of the capsule, it will work with your skirt and your pants. If the evening colors are related to the colors in your daytime capsule, your evening jacket may work with some of those pieces, too. In the color plan we've chosen, your jacket may be in burgundy, in a dressy fabric such as velvet, silk, or satin. The shape, of course, must work with the other pieces; a simple cardigan style generally works best. In this Capsule, we'll use a burgundy velvet cardigan.

Teamed with your pants this outfit can look very attractive, whether for dinner, dancing, or to a party with friends. The pants can be in burgundy or white, in silk, wool, or crepe, or they can be in burgundy velvet. Although the dressier fabrics will have a decidedly evening look, trousers in wool, of course, can be used for day as well as night and may be more practical for your needs. For this evening Capsule, we'll include trousers in white wool crepe.

On other occasions, you might wear your jacket with your skirt. Your skirt can be in any fabric from wool to matching velvet, winter white or burgundy. If you do not enjoy wearing pants, you might choose two skirts for your capsule, one in burgundy velvet (which could give you a suit look with a matching jacket), the other in white wool, for a very different look. Either one is a very effective combination, and here we'll choose burgundy wool crepe for the skirt.

To work with these pieces, you will need two dressy tops. They could be two blouses or a sweater and a blouse. For the evening, fabrics such as silk, satin, or georgette have a special appeal. While your blouse can be as tailored as a shirt, it can also be as romantic as a ruffled poet's blouse. For color, white or cream will give you the greatest adaptability. A ruffled white silk shirt can work as well with a tweed skirt during the day as it can with velvet pants at night. Your second top might be another blouse—perhaps more tailored if the first one is very soft, or more dramatic (as for example, one that is shot with lurex). You might prefer an evening sweater, one that's beaded, embroidered, or glitter trimmed.

Another approach to an evening Capsule is to work around two strong colors, such as copper and navy. Using pants in navy silk and a skirt in copper silk, you can create a totally different feeling for evening, getting even further away from your daytime dressing. The pants and skirt will become the basic foundation on which to build different looks.

Three tops can complete the picture. Two of them could be silk tunics, one in the same copper, the other in navy. They can be teamed with the matching bottoms or worn with the opposite color for a really dramatic effect. On the other hand, you may want to have two very different tops, one a tunic blouse, and the other a striped sweater. For the third top, you might choose something totally different—for example, an ivory ruffled shirt or a lace blouse that can be worn with the pants as well as with the skirt.

THE PROBLEM

Liz A. worked for a large advertising agency in their midtown office. She often went on dates directly from work, going out for drinks or dinner. The women in her office dressed very casually during the day, mostly in pants with just a blouse or sweater. Many of them lived nearby and could change before they went out in the evening. But Liz lived nearly an hour away by train and it was not usually possible for her to go home first before a date. She wanted to look more dressed up in the evening, but still be casual during the day.

THE SOLUTION

Liz had several pairs of pants that she wore to work, including navy trousers and wine trousers in wool, plus some corduroys and jeans. She also had a navy wool skirt. We built a Capsule around navy and wine and decided to save the corduroys and jeans for the week-ends. Wearing solid color blouses and low heeled shoes she could be very comfortable in the office. But we found that by keeping a pair of navy slingbacks in her desk drawer, along with one or two pretty silk scarves, she could dress up her blouse and pants for the evening and look more special for her dates.

Navy/Wine Working Capsule

	Colors			
	Navy	Wine	Accents	Will work with
A. Jacket	Trousers			All shirts and sweater
B. Pants		Trousers		All shirts and sweater
C. Skirt	Pleated			All shirts and sweater
D. Sweater		Pullover		All pants and skirt
E. Blouse			White shirt	All pants and skirt
F. Pants			Ivory shirt	All pants and skirt
G. Blouse	Shirt			All pants and skirt
H. Blouse		Shirt		All pants and skirt

Accessories

	Navy	Wine	Accents	Will work with
Shoes	Slingbacks			Everything
Handbag		Envelope		Everything
Scarves	Oblong		Floral square, Plaid square	Everything

THE PROBLEM

Sandy L. worked as a producer for a television station. Her job demanded a great deal of physical work and the ability to get around to places very fast. In fact, her working uniform was jeans, a sweatshirt and sneakers. But her husband, who was a publicity agent, often had to entertain clients in the evening and wanted Sandy to be with him. Many of the dinners and parties they went to were very dressy. Sandy didn't want to spend a lot of time thinking about what to wear when she rushed home at night to change. At the same time, the other women usually went to great trouble to look terrific, and Sandy wanted to look good too. In fact, she enjoyed dressing up and looking very feminine in the evening as opposed to her daytime jeans.

THE SOLUTION

We planned an evening Capsule around black and white separates, with three bottom pieces that could get a lot of mileage. These were a black silk skirt, a long black velvet skirt, which she already had, and a pair of black crepe pants. Then she bought two jackets, one in black velvet, the other a white chenille sweater with gold lurex trim. She had four tops, a white ruffled silk blouse and a black silk V neck blouse which she already owned, and she bought a white silk tunic top and a black sweater. Any of the tops and jackets could be worn with any of the bottoms. The thirty six combinations created from these nine pieces went from casually dressy to formal black tie, a complete evening wardrobe.

Black/White Evening Capsule

	Colors			
	Black	**White**	**Accents**	**Will work with**
A. Jacket	Velvet cardigan			All skirts and pants
B. Jackets		Chenille sweater		All skirts and pants
C. Skirt	Silk pleated			All jackets, blouses and sweater
D. Skirt	Long velvet			All jackets, blouses and sweater
E. Pants	Crepe trousers			All jackets, blouses and sweater
F. Blouse		Ruffled silk		All skirts and pants
G. Blouse	V neck silk			All skirts and pants
H. Blouse		Silk tunic		All skirts and pants
I. Sweater	Pullover			All skirts and pants

Accessories

Shoes	Satin pumps			Everything
Handbag			Gold box	Everything

THE DRESS-AND-JACKET LOOK

If you prefer dresses to separates, the Capsule Concept applies as well. Here again, a dressy jacket can be an important item. The dress and jacket approach is as workable for evening as it is for daytime. For this Capsule, black and royal blue would make an interesting combination. Beginning with the jacket, you might select a black velvet jacket in a cardigan style. It should work with any of the dresses you pick. A black crepe dress with a simple neckline can be worn for many occasions from the most low-keyed dinner to the most sophisticated party. A second dress in royal blue silk can be equally effective. This dress might be in a shirt style or might have a bow neck. A third dress in black velvet can be deliciously dramatic.

What about mixing dresses and separates for your evening Capsule? In this case, again, five pieces can be the basic components: a dress, a skirt, a jacket, and two tops. This time we'll work with brown and gold. The dress you choose could be in gold silk, in a shirt style, with a bow neck, or just a simple jewel neckline. The skirt might be in brown velvet. To work with either of these you may add a brown velvet jacket that can be worn with the silk dress and create an evening suit look with the skirt. Two tops can be worn with the skirt. One may be a white blouse, in a dressy fabric such as silk, satin, or georgette. This blouse can be in a soft, very feminine style or you may prefer a more tailored shirt style. The other top could be a sweater—one in gold lurex, for example. The skirt and tops can be worn with or without the jacket for very different effects.

ACCESSORIZING YOUR EVENING CAPSULE

It is accessories that often make the dramatic difference between a daytime and an evening look. The same dress worn toned down for day can look smashing at night when teamed with the right shoes, belt, jewelry, or scarf. One pair of evening shoes may be all you need. They can be in suede, in silk or in a dressy kidskin such as a metallic. The same applies for an evening purse—one is all you need for your Capsule, and it can be as simple as a small quilted bag with a shoulder chain or as different as a hand-sized sculptured box. As with your daytime purse, it may even slide into your briefcase for occasions when you know you'll be going out straight from the office.

Scarves and belts can add dazzle to the simplest outfit. A glittery scarf can add a glamorous touch, and a soft bow in bright silk can add a dash of drama. A tartan taffeta bow or a velvet ribbon tied under the collar can look beguilingly innocent. A gold belt or one in black suede can give a number of different looks. Black wool pants worn with a white silk shirt and a gold leather belt will give a very tailored, understated look. Team that same shirt and pants with cumberbund and a velvet jacket and you have spiced it with a flavor of flamenco.

One set of evening jewelry is all you need to start off your Capsule. It may include the same pieces you use during the day. Certainly, your watch, bracelet, earrings, and pearls can stay the same. But you might want to add something special for the evening, perhaps a glittery pair of earrings or a fabulous set of pearls.

Several years ago I came across a wonderful pearl necklace—strand after strand of pearls, finished at either end with a large rhinestone studded tassle. At the time, the price seemed outrageous, sixty-five dollars for costume jewelry. After some thought, I decided to splurge. The dozens of times I've worn this necklace, and the endless compliments it draws, reminds me so often what a bargain it really was.

A pair of fabulous fake earrings from Kenneth Jay Lane proved to be equally successful. Done in gold with pave rhinestones, they too cost far more than what I usually paid for earrings. But they work with everything from a dinner suit to a ball gown, and it doesn't matter if they're real or not—they look great.

The joy of evening clothes is that you can be as dramatic as you dare. Sometimes one outrageous item—and it doesn't have to be expensive—can be the basis of an evening Capsule. Combine it with complementary pieces, as suggested in the following two charts, and you'll have an evening wardrobe that is versatile and distinctive.

Burgundy/Winter White Evening Capsule

	Colors			Will work with
	Burgundy	**Winter White**	**Accents**	
A. Jacket	Velvet cardigan			Skirt and pants
B. Skirt	Crepe pleated			Jacket, blouse, and sweater
C. Pants		Crepe		Jacket, blouse, and sweater
D. Blouse		Crepe		Skirt and pants
E. Sweater	Pullover			Skirt and pants

Accessories

Shoes	Slingbacks			Everything
Handbag	Envelope			Everything
Earrings			Pearl/gold button	Everything
Necklace			Pearls	Everything
Bracelet			Gold	Everything
Scarf	Silk oblong		Lurex and Winter White striped oblong	Everything, at neck or waist
Belt	Patent		Gold	Everything

Evening Capsule

Black/Royal Blue

	Black	Royal Blue	Accents	Will work with
Jacket	Velvet cardigan			All dresses
Jacket	Crepe			Jacket or on its own
Dress		Silk, bow neck		Jacket or on its own
Dress	Velvet			Jacket or on its own

Accessories

	Black		Accents	Will work with
Shoes	Slingback			Everything
Handbag			Gold Evening purse	Everything
Earrings			Pearl and Gold	Everything
Necklace			Pearls	Everything
Bracelet			Gold	Everything
Scarves			Black/Gold Oblong, Red	Everything
Scarves			Oblong, Floral Square	Everything

Copper/Navy Evening Capsule

	Colors			Will work with
	Copper	Navy	Accents	
A. Skirt	Silk			Both blouses and sweater
B. Pants		Silk		Both blouses and sweater
C. Blouse		Silk tunic with self-sash		Skirt and pants
D. Blouse			Ivory ruffled	Skirt and pants
E. Sweater	Striped cardigan Copper/navy			Skirt and pants

Accessories

Shoes			Gold sandals	Everything
Handbag			Gold evening bag	Everything
Earrings			Gold button	Everything
Necklace			Gold pendant on silk cord	Everything, as a necklace, pine (without the silk and) or belt
Bracelet			Gold	Everything
Scarves			Paisley, lurex	Blouse and tunic, at neck or waist
Belt	Gold			

Brown/Gold Evening Capsule

	Brown	Gold	Accents	Will work with
Jacket	Velvet cardigan			Skirt and dress
Skirt	Velvet dirndl			Jacket, blouse and sweater
Blouse			White satin	Skirt
Sweater		Lurex knit pullover		Skirt
Dress		Silk shirtdress		Jacket or on its own

Accessories

	Brown	Gold	Accents	Will work with
Shoes		Pump		Everything
Handbag		Evening purse		Everything
Belts	Sash	Narrow		Everything
Scarves	Brown/Gold Stripe, floral, plaid			Everything
Watch		Gold band		Everything
Earrings		Pearl/Gold		Everything
Necklace			Pearls	Everything
Bracelet		Gold bangles		Everything

REAL PEOPLE

There are lifestyles that demand as much from an evening wardrobe as from a daytime one. The two women in this chapter must juggle their clothing Capsules to work from morning to night.

Both women have solid suggestions on building an evening Capsule, working around favorite colors and selecting styles that last for a long time.

Lenore Benson

Lenore Benson travels around the country giving fashion shows and seminars on the latest looks. She'll tell you the biggest trends, what's in, what's out, and what's coming. But as for herself, she says, "I don't want to look outdated. I can't. But for me being trendy doesn't work."

She's the woman in charge of promotions for *Vogue,* the one you're likely to see at a major store giving fashion ideas and advice to anyone who wants it. But Lenore makes it clear that it's style, more than fashion, that makes a woman attractive.

Round faced, with ginger hair, green eyes, and a peaches and cream complexion, Lenore has learned her own look, set her own style. "I'm five foot six and plump. I just always have a weight problem. I wear a size twelve or a size fourteen. My strongest assets are my hair, skin, and eyes, so I like to use those colors.

"In these days of components, with all of the pieces that work for you, you do a lot better if you stay within a color palette. It makes it a lot easier. If I look in my closet, and see that everything is in the same general color range, I can pull things out easily and make them go together."

This fashion professional has made color her signature. "I used to be known as a peach lady," she says, referring to her years at *Mademoiselle*. Then she introduced shades of tobacco to work with the peaches. Lately, she has brought in black and ivory, another combination that can use peach accents.

How does Lenore make her wardrobe work for her? With a work day that often extends into the night, she's got to have clothes that are versatile. The day we talked she was making an overnight trip to Philadelphia, combining business and pleasure at a farewell party for a good friend who was moving from one store to another. She had to be dressed for a day at the office, but she wouldn't have time to change before the party. She was wearing silk separates from Calvin Klein in a combination of tobacco and peach. "This silk jacket, skirt, and shirt move well from day to night. This evening when I go out to dinner my outfit will be fine." But she also wasn't taking much clothing with her for the return trip home. She told me, "I deliberately wore a jacket that reverses. I can wear it on the other side tomorrow morning when I come back on the train and go right to work. At least I'll feel like I've got something different on." She keeps her baggage to a minimum. As for carrying her personal things, she says, "My makeup and jewelry and some work I have to do are all packed in this woven straw bag that I use as my summer briefcase."

In an industry where parties are serious business, an evening wardrobe is essential. "In this business there are a lot of demands on you to appear in the evening at some big event, from a cocktail party to a charity dinner." But Lenore has found a solution. "In recent years I've been going to black tie functions in simple black dresses and changing the jewelry." Black makes a striking contrast against her pale skin, and that look has brought her many compliments. "Suddenly people started saying, 'gee, you really look good in black.'" She's been so pleased with the response, she's started buying it for her day clothes, too.

As for a problem that many women face at cocktail parties, she has learned to balance her act. "I think a huge handbag gets in the way at cocktail parties," says Lenore, "so I carry a little leather bag with a shoulder strap. That way I can manipulate it, shake a hand, and hold a drink."

With her simple clothes, it isn't surprising that jewelry is a special love. Her favorite pieces of carnelians, ambers and corals, go with the same color palettes. She finds she can still use the ambers with her new black things. "On the other hand," she says, "I find myself investing in good gold."

But it isn't only jewelry that she sees as a long term investment. "We must think investment when we buy clothes," she says. Not only because of the cost but also because of the effect. "Visability means women have to think more about how they come across." Day or night, Lenore Benson comes across as a woman with good fashion sense.

 ## Lenore Benson: Evening Capsule

Colors—Tobacco/Peach. Black/Cream. Stays mostly with shades that complement her own coloring: red hair, green eyes, peaches and cream skin.

Fabrics—Silks. Knits. Natural fibers. Lightweight fabrics that can be layered. Likes Reversibles.

Accessories—Enjoys wearing jewelry and collecting it, especially ambers and carnelians. Victorian pieces. Gold.

Style—Smart but not trendy. Earthy.

Key words—Style. Ease. Energy. Robust.

Susan Samuels

When Susan Samuels was in Sierra Leone as wife of the American Ambassador her life involved a blending of cultures and constant entertaining, from luncheons to frequent black tie dinners. "As an ambassador's wife, I tended to wear a lot of long things," she says. Now that she is back in the States, she still goes out to dinner about four nights a week, but they are not as formal. "I like to keep things for a very long time," she explained "and when I came home, I simply cut the hems of my long gowns. Now they're perfect as dinner dresses."

As Executive Producer for Living Theater, the national outreach company of Arena Stage, one of the country's oldest resident theater companies, she has helped raise hundreds of thousands of dollars. "We go to everything from theater openings to embassy dinner parties to casual evenings with friends." The people are as varied as theatrical producers, business leaders, ambassadors, and art dealers. About seventy percent of these functions call for dressy clothes, twenty percent are definitely casual, and another ten percent are black tie.

Except for the occasional charity ball which requires an evening gown, Susan works around an evening Capsule of black and white. With her tiny size-four figure, she can make great buys. In her Capsule, the pieces go from a short black lace dress by Bill Blass (bought on sale at Lord & Taylor), to a white silk suit bought at a theatrical auction. "The suit was designed for Blanche Du Bois in *Streetcar Named Desire*. It is extraordinarily useful. It can be toned down with a simple silk blouse. On the other hand, I have a plum colored halter wrap top that I wear with it. That makes it very dressy." Her other basic pieces include a black silk skirt, a soft white silk skirt, and two pairs of silk gabardine trousers, one in black and one in white. Several dressy sweaters—including a black sweater set shot with silver, and a striped lurex set in silver, gold and bronze—work with the various skirts and pants. In addition, she also has some silk blouses for variety.

Much of her evening wardrobe can be worn for daytime, too. For example, Susan says, "I can wear my black skirt with a simple white silk shirt for a meeting during the day, come home, take off the silk blouse and black leather pumps and switch to the sweaters and dressy shoes. Then I'm ready to go out for the evening." She adds, "A lot of what I do is based on separates for day and night."

Changing her accessories is often the way she transforms an outfit from a daytime to an evening look. "Shoes are what often change a wardrobe for evening," she says. She has three pair of dressy pumps, one in gold, one in silver, and one in black suede. She feels that jewelry is also very important for the evening. "During the day I usually wear just small gold hoop earrings. But for evening I have a number of good earrings to accent whatever I'm wearing. I like rings at night, too, but never in the day."

Not too long ago Susan gave a dinner for thirty people, including several ambassadors, well-known journalists, and political leaders. Although she did most of the cooking herself and needed to be dressed comfortably enough to move around the kitchen, she also wanted to appear as an elegant hostess. What did she wear? "I wanted to wear pants so that I could bend and get around easily. I used my white flannel trousers that I wear winter and summer, daytime or evening, and dressed them up with my striped lurex sweater set. My gold kid pumps were perfect to carry through the dressy look, and I finished it off with gold earrings and a gold kid belt." Though, in fact, most of the pieces could have been worn during the day, it was the gold shoes that gave her a special evening look. "I don't remember when I received so many compliments," Susan says, "and I think it may have been because it was all so easy, and I felt so comfortable in my clothes."

 Susan Samuels: Evening Capsule

Colors—Black/White.

Fabrics—Silk gabardine. Wool crepe. Wool flannel. Silk crepe. Touches of metallics. Likes fabrics that can be worn year round, that move easily from day to night.

Accessories—Counts on them for drama at night. Feels shoes make the biggest change. Lots of different earrings for evening; rings, too. Likes flowing scarves, dressy belts.

Style—Depends on separates for lots of looks.

Key words—Drama. Glitter. Theatrical without theatrics.

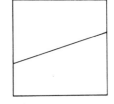 *Chapter 5*

THE TRAVEL CAPSULE:

Some people go away for a weekend and look as if they'll be gone for a month. Others can go from London to Luxor for three weeks with one suitcase and an overnight bag. How to select the Capsule pieces, what to take and what to leave behind, plus how to pull out the best from your different Capsules are all important parts of the travel picture. With the right clothing, two pairs of shoes can do where four might otherwise be needed—or you might take more shirts and fewer skirts, a sweater rather than a jacket, or some smashing piece of jewelry instead of a second evening outfit. Some fabrics travel well from hot climates to cold. Others may be drip dry but leaving you wringing wet in the desert. Silks and lightweight wools in cool colors can be better travelmates than any shade of polyester. On the other hand, one down filled coat can keep you toasty warm when the only heat you have is coming from a campfire. That same quilted coat can look as chic in Paris as in Peru.

THINK BEFORE YOU PACK

Business trips have become a standard part of the working woman's life. What do you take with you—and even more important, what do you leave at home? First, the basic questions must be answered. Where are you going? How long will you be there? And what will you be doing? What will the weather be like? Some newspapers (such as the *New York Times*) give a smattering of reports from cities all over the U.S. and around the world. Some television meteorologists give a rundown on weather conditions across the country. If these are not helpful, call ahead. By telephoning Information in any U.S. city (using the area code plus 555-1212) you can get the number for the recorded local weather bulletin. Calling ahead for a local report may cost a little extra, but it can save you a lot of aggravation.

Studying your schedule before you pack will give you a good idea of how many changes you will need. Breakfast, lunch and dinner with the same people for several days will mean more changes than one meeting each day with different people and dinner in your room in front of the television. Thinking in terms of changes helps clarify your needs. Four days and four nights in one town can mean eight changes. Your itinerary is a good starting point for packing.

FLEXIBILITY IS THE KEY

After you've determined what the weather will be like and what you will be doing, it's time to decide what to take. If you have kept your wardrobe to one basic Capsule, this group becomes your travel Capsule as well. If you have two or more Capsules, you may simply choose the one that will work for you. Or you may bring together pieces from two different Capsules whose colors are compatible.

Like any other Capsule, the one for travel works on the two-color system with pieces that interrelate. The best travel Capsule has the fewest number of pieces and the greatest amount of flexibility. It should require only one color in shoes and handbags. With the exception of very formal occasions, the clothes you take should function well for day and night.

As Fashion Director of Garfinckel's, my job required that I be in constant contact with the market. That meant frequent travel to New York (thirty trips a year, each for a minimum of two days), and two three-week trips a year to the European fashion capitals of Paris, London, and Milan. There were occasional trips to other U.S. and European cities as well. The trips to Seventh Avenue usually involved being with different people from the store every day. I might be working on fall promotions with the coat buyer one day, and on spring shows with the designer sportswear buyer the next. Working with different people meant less of a need for changes. The quick trips to New York became like a commuter's shuttle for me, and I usually traveled with just a carry-on bag. The European trips meant eighteen days and eighteen evenings with exactly the same people all the time. For these I took a suitcase plus a carry-on bag. In both situations, I worked around travel Capsules.

For a three day trip to New York, I might take a Black/Gray Capsule. This would include a gray striped two-piece silk dress I would wear on the plane with a black wool sweater jacket. I would pack a black knife-pleated skirt in wool crepe and a gray flannel skirt, one silk blouse in ivory, and a pullover in black. The dress could stand on its own if I were going out to dinner, and look right for work with the sweater jacket. The blouse of the dress could be worn with any of the skirts. The black sweater jacket also worked with the other skirts and made a suit look with the black one. The pullover went with all of the skirts and had the look of a dress when combined with the black skirt, giving me another dressy outfit if I were going out in the evening again. The ivory blouse, of course, worked with any of the skirts on its own and with either sweater. The simple black shoes I took—one pair which I wore, and one pair which I packed—went with everything. My basic accessories included a pair of gold earrings, a pair of pearl earrings, a rope of pearls, and a black leather belt. I always wore my watch and gold bracelet. At the bottom of my bag I kept a black nylon raincoat that took up almost no space at all. A few pieces of lingerie, a cosmetic bag and electric rollers finished the picture.

It was always fun to see what other people from the store took when they traveled. Joan Carl, who was the buyer of designer clothes, traveled to Europe with me. We usually carried the same amount of luggage, but the contents was totally different. While I have dark hair and skin, she is a pale blonde with a very fair complexion. Our color preferences were always dissimilar. In fact, we used this contrast as a guideline for our customers' tastes. At the Missoni show-room just outside Milan, color was abundant everywhere—from the flowers blooming indoors and out, to the food, to, of course, the clothes, which were rich in complex color combinations. The range offered by the Missoni collections was enormous, but we finally worked out a system of selecting two color groupings, one Joan's choice for blondes and redheads, and one my choice for brunettes. Though our choice of styles was usually similar, the effect of the clothes in different colors offered a marked contrast.

Before Joan travels to Europe, she lines everything up in her office. Then she makes sure there isn't anything she can't wear at least three ways. A pair of pants must be able to work with a sweater and two blouses, a skirt must do the same, a jacket must go with all of the bottoms. Whatever she takes must have that kind of flexibility. Otherwise, no matter how much she loves it, it stays home. As for colors, she might base her Capsule around a favorite knit coat that has purple and burgundy in it. She might include a purple knit two-piece dress, a three piece striped knit outfit, lots of silk blouses in purple, wine, and ivory, a pair of burgundy suede pants and a purple suede skirt. Mixing the sweater knits with the suedes gives one interesting look, while combining the suedes and the silks gives a totally different texture. Again, there are enough color combinations and styles to give her good flexibility. Even if some things are at the hotel cleaners, she knows she has clothes in her closet that will work together.

There are some trips that require pulling together different Capsules to form your travel Capsule. For example, one trip I made to Europe included the usual stops in Milan, Florence, Paris, and London, but then I was meeting my journalist-husband for a trip to Egypt and an interview with President Anwar Sadat. It was April, and it would still be rather chilly in Europe. In Cairo and Luxor, however, the temperature could climb as high as 115 degrees. I needed to combine a winter Capsule and a summer Capsule.

For this particular trip, I chose to work around a Capsule of Green/Ivory. From my winter Capsule, I packed a suit in a forest green wool tweed. Then I added a two-piece dark green silk paisley shirtdress. With these I packed an ivory pull-over sweater, a rust turtleneck, and two ivory silk blouses (one with a notched collar and one with a bow). The rest of the clothing came from my summer Capsule and included a two-piece raw silk shirtdress in rust, a one-piece shirt-dress in ivory, and an ivory silk-and-wool-blend suit. For evening I included a pair of ivory crepe trousers. I did throw in a pair of jeans for sightseeing in Egypt, and they came in handy for some casual evenings on the Left Bank in Paris, too. A rust unlined coat kept me warm, and on very chilly days I could layer my sweaters under my suits. For wet days, I had my nylon raincoat. I took three pairs of shoes—beige pumps, rust pumps, and beige espadrilles for sightseeing expeditions in Cairo and Luxor. I carried a tan leather clutch bag during the day, but I did take a small antique Japanese basketweave purse for dressy evenings. All of this fit in one suitcase. My personal items went in a carry-on bag, so that my luggage was manageable no matter where I was, For me, it was a truly complete travel Capsule.

Before I pack for any trip, I take out the pieces I want and spread them on the bed. Then I make sure that each piece can be used in several different ways. Only then does it go in the suitcase. There are some essentials I know I'll always take with me, and I keep them on a separate shelf in my bathroom cabinet. They include a separate set of makeup in small plastic containers, a hand steamer for domestic travel, a set of electric rollers and a small blow dryer, both of which can change current automatically for international trips. I travel with nylon lingerie which takes up very little space and can be rinsed out and hung to dry overnight. I do always pack a lightweight robe since I enjoy calling room service for some of my dinners. In fact, that's one luxury I look forward to when I travel!

DESIGNING YOUR OWN TRAVEL CAPSULE

Suppose there is a trip coming up in your schedule. How should you go about selecting the clothes to pack? First decide on a color scheme. That way you can automatically eliminate pieces that won't work. Then decide which are the most important events on your schedule and how you want to look. If you are taking a suit, consider it as a separate skirt and jacket as well. Then pick other pieces that will relate—another top that will work with the skirt and other skirts or pants that will go with the jacket. You might include a dress that also can work with the jacket. For a two- or three-day trip, one jacket and two skirts or one jacket, pants and a skirt (all in a dark color) may be enough. While the skirt and jacket together give an excellent authoritative look, the skirt alone can be dressed up for evening with a pretty blouse. The pants can be very comfortable for traveling and can also function as an evening look. If you are choosing dresses, include at least one jacket that can work with them so that again, you can get a crisper look for meetings and a softer look when you want it.

Keep to solid colors or subtle patterns in jackets, pants, skirts, and dresses. This gives you more flexibility. Prints can get pretty tiresome if you're going to be away for any length of time. They are more recognizable, and not as flexible to work with. But you can introduce color and pattern with blouses, sweaters, and scarves. Blouses, indeed, are a great way to change mood and color easily, without taking up much space in your suitcase. Scarves, another small item to take, pack a lot of punch in terms of color and effect. A white shirt and a dark skirt can take on a dozen different looks depending on the scarf that is worn with it.

If you enjoy jewelry, it can have the same effect, changing the look of an outfit so that it becomes something new and fresh looking even though you've been wearing it a lot more than you would have if you were home. A rope of pearls automatically dresses up your silk blouse and skirt. A big necklace adds drama to a simple sweater and skirt. It's this kind of change that can keep your travel wardrobe interesting.

The essential accessories must travel, too; they are part of your Capsule. That means that your shoes and handbag must work with all of your clothes. For short trips, two pairs of shoes should do the trick, one that you wear and one that you pack. Longer periods away may warrant three pairs, two for the daytime and a dressy pair for evening. If any sightseeing trips will be included, you may need an additional pair of walking shoes. In any case, no more than four pairs of shoes should be necessary, one of which you'll be wearing. Your handbag should complement all of your clothes; however, if you are planning any dressy evenings you will want to include one evening purse.

There are some business trips that allow time for leisure, whether it's sight-seeing, sun worshipping or shopping. Along with a swimsuit, include a pair of casual pants or a casual skirt. It should be in the color scheme of your travel Capsule so that it can work with the tops you take along. If there are any dressy evenings planned, one simple dress, in a jersey or a silk crepe, should be sufficient. Or, you may include a dressy pair of slacks and a pretty top.

Short trips may only require an overnight case for all of your things. But for longer stays, one hanging bag or suitcase should accommodate all of your clothes. Hanging bags have the advantage of arriving when you do, and keep your clothing hung while you travel. Your personal items, however, are always safest in a separate carry-on bag. That sinking feeling that comes when you arrive and find your luggage lost is even worse when you find yourself without makeup, curlers, or whatever else you need to make you, you. One bag and a carry-on gives you the ability to handle your things without the help of porters—who may not be there anyway. If you anticipate making any pur-chases along the way, slip a separate nylon bag into your suitcase. It will take up almost no space at all and will allow you to shop without worrying about crushing your clothes on the trip back. If you do buy any clothes, remember your Capsule.

THE PROBLEM

Kathleen H. was a publicist for a small firm in San Francisco. The head of the company asked if she would be interested in going to London for two weeks on business. She was delighted but realized that her wardrobe needed some embellishing. At work she wore very casual clothes, but in London she would need a dressier look.

THE SOLUTION

Kathleen had a bright navy jacket which she liked very much. She also owned a white pleated skirt, and had recently bought a raspberry silk blouse. She wanted to work around these clothes. We added a pair of wine pants, a navy skirt, a two-piece dress in navy and wine silk, a wine cardigan, and a navy blouse. She could attend meetings during the day, go out to dinner and the theater in the evening, and pack just ten pieces of clothing.

Navy/Wine Travel Capsule
Two-Week Trip

	Navy	Wine	Accents	Will work with
Jacket	Blazer			Skirts, pants, and dresses
Skirt	pleated			Jackets, all blouses and sweater
Skirt			White pleated	Blazer to make suit
Skirt	Checked dirndl Navy/wine			Checked shirt to make dress
Pants		Trousers		All tops
Blouse	Checked print shirt, bow neck Navy/wine			Skirts and pants
Blouse	Shirt			Skirts and pants
Blouse		Bow neck		Skirts and pants
Sweater		Cardigan		Skirts and pants

Checklist

	Robe (Lightweight)
	Sleepwear
	Underwear
	Cosmetics
	Hair dryer
	Travel curlers
	Hand steamer
	Medicine
	Sports equipment

Accessories

	Navy	Wine	Accents	
Shoes	Pump	Pump	Shoes	
Handbag	Shoulder bag	Clutch		
Belts	Narrow	Narrow		
Scarves	Oblong	Pocket Square	Multi-stripe, Floral square	
Watch			Gold	
Earrings			Gold, Pearl	
Necklace			Gold, Pearls	
Bracelet			Gold	

THE PROBLEM

Sharon T. lived in Boston and worked for an electronics firm. The industry was holding a convention in Atlanta. Sharon would be representing the company at the booth during the day and would be going to dinners and parties in the evening. She needed clothes that would be comfortable and could be dressed up at night.

THE SOLUTION

Working around a favorite ivory suit, Sharon used that as the jacket and skirt. She decided to buy a pair of ivory pants, as they would be perfect during the summer, too. She took an ivory blouse, a red silk shirt, and a teal silk shirt and skirt which would mix well with the ivory skirt and pants. To make another interesting look, she also brought along a new purple cardigan. With this Ivory/Teal Capsule, she was able to get several varied looks from ivory mono-tones to bursting brights.

Ivory/Teal Travel Capsule

Four Day Convention

	Ivory	Teal	Accents	Will work with
Jacket	Blazer			Skirts and pants Ivory skirt to make suit.
Skirt		Pleated		All blouses, jacket and sweater. Teal blouse to make suit.
Skirt	Slim			Jacket, all blouses and sweater.
Pants	Trousers			Jacket, blouses, and sweater.
Blouse		Shirt		Skirts and pants
Blouse			Ivory shirt	Skirts and pants
Blouse			Red shirt	Skirts and pants
Sweater			Purple Cardigan	Skirts and pants

Checklist

	Robe (Lightweight)
	Sleepwear
	Underwear
	Cosmetics
	Hair dryer
	Travel curlers
	Hand steamer
	Medicine
	Sports equipment

Accessories

Shoes	Pump, Slingback			
Handbag	Clutch			
Belts	Narrow		Gold	
Scarves			Teal/red Floral oblong, Red/ivory/polka dot	
Watch			Gold	
Earrings			Gold, Pearl	
Necklace			Gold, Pearls	
Bracelet			Gold	

HOW TO PACK

Packing a hanging bag is quite simple—whatever you would ordinarily hang, such as jackets, skirts and dresses, are hung in the bag. Folded items, such as sweaters and nightgowns, go in the bottom compartments along with all of your other personal items. Because this type of luggage goes on the plane with you, you can also include your cosmetics and other essentials in it without having to worry about their getting lost. So, a hanging bag can give you a great sense of independence, freeing you from worries about lost luggage, eliminating the necessity of waiting around for your bags long after you have disembarked from the airplane, and enabling you to carry your own suitcase.

If you prefer a traditional suitcase, which, of course can hold more than a hanging bag can, you should still be able to put all of your clothes and accessories into one bag. There are several travel items you might consider which can make packing easier. One is a jewelry roll, which can hold necklaces, bracelets, pins and earrings and protect them from getting damaged. There are also attractive lingerie cases which hold nightgowns, panties, bras and slips, and which can be hung in the closet upon your arrival at your hotel. Plastic lined cosmetic cases are the ideal way to carry cosmetics as well as medicine, nail polish, soap, sewing kit, and any other items which you consider essential. Plain plastic bags are also handy for holding shoes, so have some of these available.

To pack your suitcase, first line up everything you are planning to take with you, making sure that your shoes and handbags will go with all of your clothes. The first layer in your bag should contain your shoes, going sole to sole, the heel of one touching the toe of the other, your handbags, your accessories, including scarves, and your intimate apparel. Use the empty spaces between bags and shoes for your softer things so that you fill out and even off that layer. On top of this will go your largest items, your skirts, pants, dresses and jackets. Your skirts should be placed flat in the bag and then folded once in half. To pack your pants, hold them by the cuffs, with one leg flat against the other. Then fold them in half. Dresses can be a little trickier to pack, but, again, one fold should be all you need, unless the skirt is very full. Hold the dress by the shoulder and place it in your suitcase so that the top of the dress is inside and the skirt is draped over the edge. Then place the sleeves across the front and fold the skirt up once over the sleeves and bodice. If the skirt is very full, fold the sides in first and then fold the whole bottom up to reach the top. Make sure the dress is buttoned, zipped and belted before you pack it, so that it retains its shape. Like the dresses, jackets should be buttoned too, then placed buttons down into the suitcase. Bring the sleeves back, and then fold over the bottom of the jacket to fit into the bag. After you have packed these items, then put in blouses, sweaters, and a raincoat, which you may need to get at quickly.

When using a suitcase that travels in the luggage compartment of the plane, take along a separate small bag that will go under your seat. In it can go cosmetics, that should be in plastic containers inside the plastic lined cosmetics case, hair dryer, electric curlers, travel iron or steamer, alarm clock, jewelry roll and perhaps a collapsible travel umbrella.

In choosing your luggage, consider the many materials now available. It is particularly important to be concerned about weight as you may often find yourself carrying your own bags. Fortunately, it is no longer necessary to buy a suitcase that is heavy even before you pack it. Although beautiful, but heavy leather luggage is still available, other options include hard-sided fabric bags, hard-sided molded bags, soft-sided canvas bags, and soft-sided featherweight bags made of parachute cloth. I have found soft-sided bags to be extremely practical as they are light to carry and can hold much more than one would imagine. Before you go, make sure your name and address are clearly marked on luggage tags attached to your bags. This is required on all airlines and can save you from picking up the wrong suitcase or help you in identifying a lost bag.

Olive/Gold Travel Capsule

Three Day Trip

	Olive	Gold	Accents	Will work with
Jacket	Tweed, Olive/Gold			Skirts and dresses
Skirt	Tweed slim, Olive/Gold			Both blouses, Tweed jacket to make suit
Skirt	Paisley print, dirndl, Olive/Gold			Both blouses and jacket.
Blouse	Paisley print Olive/Gold			Both skirts will make dress with paisley dirndl
Blouse		Shirt		Both skirts
Dress	Sweater, knit			Jacket or on its own

Checklist

	Robe (Lightweight)
	Sleepwear
	Underwear
	Cosmetics
	Hair dryer
	Travel curlers
	Hand steamer
	Medicine
	Sports equipment

Accessories

	Olive	Gold	Accents	
Shoes			Wine pumps Wine slingback	
Handbag	Wine envelope			
Belts	·		Wine narrow	
Scarves	Olive/Gold stripe square		Wine oblong	
Watch			Gold band	
Earrings			Gold ball	
Necklace			Gold beads	
Bracelet			Gold bangle	

Ivory/Tan Travel Capsule
Three Day Trip

	Ivory	Tan	Accents	Will work with
Jacket	Blazer			Pants, make suit with skirt
Skirt	Slim			Jacket, blouses and sweater
Pants		Trouser		Jacket, blouses and sweater
Blouse	Shirt			Skirt and pants
Blouse		V neck shirt		Skirt and pants
Sweater			Rust cardigan	Skirt and pants

Checklist

	Robe (Lightweight)
	Sleepwear
	Underwear
	Cosmetics
	Hair dryer
	Travel curlers
	Hand steamer
	Medicine
	Sports equipment

Accessories

Shoes		Pump, slingback		Everything
Handbag		Clutch		Everything
Belts		Narrow		Everything
Scarves		Brown plaid Rust floral, rust oblong		Everything
Watch		Leather band		Everything
Earrings			Gold	Everything
Necklace			Gold, amber beads	Everything
Bracelet			Gold	Everything

Navy/Gray Travel Capsule
One-Week Convention

	Navy	Gray	Accents	Will work with
Jacket	Blazer			Skirts, pants, and dresses
Jacket			Red cardigan	Skirts, pants, and dresses
Skirt	Pleated			All jackets, blouses and sweater. Blazer to make suit
Skirt		Dirndl, paisley print, Navy/Gray/Red		All jackets, blouses and sweater. Paisley shirt to make dress
Pants		Trousers		All jackets, blouses and sweater.
Blouse		Paisley print shirt, bow neck		Skirts and pants
Blouse			Ivory shirt	Skirts and pants
Blouse		Bow neck		Skirts and pants
Sweater			Red pullover	Skirts and pants
Dress	Shirtdress			Jackets or on its own
Active wear			Shorts, T-shirt	
Active wear			Swimsuit	

Checklist

	Robe (Lightweight)
	Sleepwear
	Underwear
	Cosmetics
	Hair dryer
	Travel curlers
	Hand steamer
	Medicine
	Sports equipment

Accessories

	Navy	Gray	Accents	
Shoes	Slingbacks Pumps		Tennis/Running shoes	
Handbag	Shoulder, Evening clutch			
Belts	Narrow		Gold	
Scarves			Multi-stripe, Floral square	
Watch			Gold	
Earrings			Gold, Pearl	
Necklace			Gold, Pearls	
Bracelet			Gold	

Forest/Ginger Travel Checklist
One-Week Trip

	Forest	Ginger	Accents	Will work with
Jacket		Blazer		All skirts and pants
Skirt		Dirndl		Blazer to make suit
Skirt	Paisley print, pleated Forest/ginger			Paisley shirt to make dress
Pants	Trousers			All jackets and blouses
Blouse	Paisley print shirt Forest/ginger			All skirts and pants
Blouse			Ivory shirt	All skirts and pants
Blouse		Shirt		All skirts and pants
Blouse	Bow neck			All skirts and pants
Sweater	Cardigan			All skirts and pants

Checklist

- Robe (Lightweight)
- Sleepwear
- Underwear
- Cosmetics
- Hair dryer
- Travel curlers
- Hand steamer
- Medicine
- Sports equipment

Accessories

	Forest	Ginger	Accents	
Shoes		Pump	Rust pump	
Handbag		Envelope		
Belts	Wide	Narrow		
Scarves	Oblong	Oblong	Mustard square	
Watch			Gold	
Earrings			Gold, Amber	
Necklace			Gold, Amber	
Bracelet			Gold	

REAL PEOPLE

For the women in this chapter, travel is a way of life. Although their trips may vary from overnight to a month long, their needs are always the same—maximum looks from minimum clothes.

Based on their capsules, these women offer some solid, practical advice on how to make travel easy and comfortable.

Trisha Wilson

Last year Trisha Wilson won an award from the American Council of Women, a tribute to her outstanding accomplishments in business and art. This year she is going to jail. Her one-day prison term is part of an experiment by the Leadership of Dallas sponsored by the local Chamber of Commerce to understand the problems of all of the citizens in the community.

At thirty-two, this perky, blonde dynamo is an active participant in city affairs and president of Trisha Wilson & Associates, an interior and architectural design firm with fifteen designers.

To create fresh ideas for a steady stream of clients, she searches for the new and different. "I've had two clients send me around the world," she says in her Texas drawl. Where did she go on her last trip? "I started in San Francisco, then to Japan, Hong Kong, Bangkok, Sri Lanka, Bombay, Zurich, Copenhagen, London, Chicago, and home." Not quite *"Around the World in Eighty Days,"* her trip lasted just two-and-a-half weeks. In that period, she went from the bitter cold of a January blizzard in Copenhagen to the sizzling equatorial heat of Sri Lanka.

What clothes do you take for a trip which has such sharp contrasts—not just in climate, but in culture? "There was no way to anticipate it. A silk dress just doesn't go on an elephant, but in the jungle they're used as taxis." For her unexpected elephant rides in search of native art, she bought a batik sundress in Sri Lanka. But for the rest of her trip, she was totally prepared, and packed everything in one foldable hanging bag. She included extra expandable bags for personal shopping along the way. "I'm a big shopper, so I wanted plenty of room to bring things back."

"I began with the shoes," she told me. "I coordinated everything with one color, navy. I took three pairs of shoes—walking shoes for day, sandals for night and one pair of boots." She also wore the sandals during the day with her sundress as well. Her handbags were in navy, too. "I had two purses—a nighttime bag and a shoulder bag, which I feel is imperative because you've always got your hands full."

The clothes themselves were minimal and basic. She worked around the theme of Navy/Gray. "I had a lightweight tropical wool skirt in navy that I could wear during the day with a silk or cotton blouse, and I had a beaded sweater I could wear with it at night." Her other skirt was in gray tropical wool. She brought along two jackets, one a blazer that she could work into a suit look with the navy skirt. The other jacket was a gray tweed with flecks of navy. That jacket had an extra bonus of her own invention. "I had my dressmaker do a quilted navy velvet collar that I could put on the collar of the jacket. That way I could make it either daytime or nighttime." She also included a pair of navy pants and a navy silk dress. "Silk takes no room at all and you can just steam it out," she says. A white silk blouse, a white cotton shirt, a paisley silk blouse, plus several wool sweaters, gave her the variety and flexibility she needed. The only other item was a navy trench coat with a button-out lining. "The reason I took a dark coat was it could go either way. It cost the same as a khaki color but it looked so much more formal at night."

With just these basic pieces, she stressed, "I never wore the same outfit twice, but I wore the same clothes every day." She explained how she changed the look with her accessories. "I took a lot of accessories because they don't take up any room. I had three different belts—a leather one, a gold one, and a striped wrap. I also had a paisley cummerbund which I could do around twice at the neck and make a bow. I had about five ties to make into bows and some scarves and a muffler."

Among the personal items Trisha packed were electric rollers and a small hair-dryer. As for her other essentials, "Elizabeth Arden has a travel kit for less than ten dollars with the nightcream and everything in it. I bought little plastic bottles for shampoo and things like that. I put all of that in one plastic bag and then in the big bag."

How did she manage with so little? "It's the only way you can do it. It's a matter of survival." How did she know it would all work? "I start out every trip with a blank sheet of paper and write down the days I'll be away. For example, I'll put down 'Monday day, Monday night, Tuesday day, etc.' " That way she sees exactly what her needs will be and writes down what she will wear. She explains her own philosophy: "I'm a prime believer that your only limitation is your imagination." Trisha has let her imagination soar, and it has taken her not only around the world but to the top of her profession as well.

 ## Trisha Wilson: Travel Capsule

Colors—Navy/Gray. Brown/Gray.

Fabrics—Lightweight and seasonless: Tropical weight wools, flannel, silk, cotton.

Accessories—Counts on scarves, bows, and belts to create varied looks. Begins with shoes and bags. Stays with one color here, then works her travel capsule around it. Loves to create ideas—a belt buckle made from an old compact.

Style—"Your only limitation is your imagination."

Key words—Original. Imaginative. Perky. Fresh.

Diane Sawyer

Diane Sawyer has a double image problem. She is concerned not only with how she wants to be seen, but also how she will look on the television screen. What may work face to face may not be successful on camera. Says this CBS network news correspondent, "Television dressing just fascinates me. Things that you think should work well don't, like a simple black suit and a simple red blouse. You come across looking like a department store inspector." It's not the image of the girl in gray flannel that Diane wants to project, but she does want to convey an air of authority. "At first glance you might think it's the duplication of a man's attire that subconsciously suggests a man's authority, but I don't think so. I think it's the completeness of it." Must there always be a jacket? "I think you can get that look with sweaters on the air," she replies. "I think a sweater that molds the shoulders has an effect similar to a jacket."

Distraction may be the biggest problem on the screen. Although Diane enjoys wearing accessories and feels they give her clothing individuality and extra mileage, she is concerned that they capture the attention of the audience. "It is the curiousness of the camera eye that picks up the extraneous item and rivets on it. The simpler, but not stark simple, the better." She may wear a pin on her sweater, but she's learned to choose simple ones, and not those with "interesting patterns in them, because then the viewer spends the whole time trying to figure out what on earth that says on your pin."

She's also used accessories to beef up her spare travel wardrobe. Covering the 1980 political campaigns, Diane was often away for two or three weeks at a time, living out of one hanging bag. "You have three or four things and you wear them every day. I had three or four looks I could get from one item, and I took about three sets of items: jackets, skirts, and shirts." How did she keep the public from getting bored? "I took a lot of different earrings. Colored earrings can make a lot of difference on television, so I took green ones, purples ones, red ones." She also took several necklaces, including brightly colored ones, neutrals and gold. She brought along a change of bracelets, too, though they don't show up as much on camera. "I also took a couple of scarves that I would work around the neck or at the waist." She packed one other morale booster— a pair of silk pants and a bright silk shirt. "I can't tell you what it did for me psychologically. When you've lived in sturdy clothes all day long, it's fantastic to put on something flamboyant."

 Diane Sawyer: Travel Capsule

Colors—White/Pretty pales.

Fabrics—Soft sweaters. Wool skirts. Silk blouses.

Accessories—Simple and nondistracting. Bright colors, in jewelry, to change a look. Scarves to wear at the neck or the waist.

Style—Separates pulled together with an accent on accessories. A soft look in a tough world.

Key words—Authoritatively feminine.

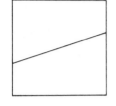

Chapter 6

SHOP TALK:

A working wardrobe is not static. As a reflection of you, it will change and develop as you do. Just as you bring to your work some of your past experience, you may bring to your wardrobe some of the clothes you already own. To build a working wardrobe will require a sifting process, selecting out those pieces which you really like and enjoy, discarding those in which you have never really felt comfortable. It is likely that there will be a number of items with which you can work. They may be the basis of one Capsule or several, depending, of course, on what they are and what colors they are in.

After deciding what to keep, the next step is filling in the missing pieces of your Capsule. For some people, shopping is not a pleasant experience, but as you know what you want, the process itself becomes much easier. Knowing the kinds of clothes you need for your Capsule and the look you want to project, will help you as you go through the stores.

LOOK BEFORE YOU BUY

Shopping should be a three-step procedure. Begin by looking through fashion magazines and fashion catalogs to give you a sense of direction. Not only will you discover what is in style, you will also see what clothes you now have that can be adapted to your new working wardrobe. Cut out pictures of what you like, whether it is a particular item, or a total look; this can help you when you are in the stores. You may even be able to do some of your shopping by telephone or by mail if you find specific items you can use for your Capsule.

The second step is also investigative. Scout the stores to see what is actually available. Although the magazines are a great inspiration, they are sometimes too advanced even for the retailers, and the items they show are not always bought from the manufacturers. In fact, each month the fashion magazines will call the leading stores around the country to inform them of the clothes to be featured in future editions and to find out which stores have actually bought these items so they can be credited with the merchandise. But all too often, fashion editors choose looks which store buyers don't feel are salable.

Actually going through the stores will give you a realistic appraisal of what is there. In addition, it will give you an opportunity to study store windows and interior displays. Take advantage of them. Store personnel take a lot of time and thought to do them, and retailers look upon them as a teaching process, a way of showing the customer the newest looks, the most important or forward merchandise, and how it can all be put together.

Once inside the store, head for the expensive areas. Why? To teach yourself what the best merchandise looks like, what trends are being shown, what colors, what fabrics, and what shapes are sure to be around for a while. If you want to know where hemlines are going, if pants will be narrow or full, if new fabrics have been developed, or if new color combinations are being worked together, this is the place to get your information. The clothing industry is like a pyramid. New ideas come from a small group of people—the designers—and from there the best looks are copied and adapted for wider and wider markets. Naturally, this filtering process takes a while, so the best of the new looks are around for a long time. If the latest trend is, for example, intricate sweaters, they may start out as hand knits costing several hundred dollars. They may be copied for several seasons at less and less money. Of course, the quality and workmanship may not be the same, but the look will be there.

While you are still scouting the stores, look around for new areas. More and more retailers are gearing themselves to the working woman. Departments are being opened with an eye to the executive suite. "The Office" at Abraham and Straus, "Corporate Image" at Filene's, and "Careers" at Marshall Field & Co. are just three examples of this trend. Shopping in these departments can save innumerable hours. They often stock clothing and accessories gathered from around the store, including merchandise priced from moderate to expensive. Often the department has a special manager, someone who is tuned in to a career woman's needs.

Many stores have personal shoppers who can become an extension of their customers, keeping track of their needs, their taste, and their budgets. They will (most often without charge although sometimes with a first time minimum), pull together the clothes you want, have them ready to be tried on at your convenience, and spend the hours you don't have hunting down those really needed items. These consultants can be a goldmine of information. They are thoroughly familiar with what is in the store and can find things quickly and easily. They usually know what is coming in to stock as well as what is going on sale. Because they work with the clothing all of the time, they know what will go with what, how to change a look from casual to dressy, and how to update last year's clothes.

While personal shoppers are particularly helpful in big stores, a knowledgeable saleswoman can be invaluable in a smaller store or within a department of a larger store. She may be the owner or just someone who understands your needs and knows not only what you may like but what will look good on you. She may even be someone who looks like you, has a similar figure or coloring, or dresses with the kind of style you admire.

THE PROBLEM
Eileen M. had lived in the same city in Ohio for most of her life. From the time she was a young girl, she had shopped in one favorite department store. Recently she had moved to Chicago, and found herself confused by all of the large department stores. She found she had neither the time nor the desire to run all over town trying to find what stores had the merchandise she wanted. But with a new job for herself and for her husband, she knew she needed some new clothes.

THE SOLUTION
Eileen called several of the major stores and found out that some of them had personal shoppers. After talking to them on the phone, she felt that one was too aggressive, one insisted on too high a minimum purchase, but the third seemed agreeable to her. Making an appointment on a lunch hour, Eileen went in and met Caroline in person. In discussing her needs, she explained that she would be going out to business dinners with her husband a good deal, and that she worked in a small office as well. Her favorite clothes at the moment were a two piece knit suit in navy and a kelly green jacket. She had a navy skirt too, that she wore a lot, but she needed to pull all of her things together plus get some dressy ideas. Caroline suggested that she could go through the store, gather some clothes together and present them to Eileen the following week working around a first time budget of $250. They agreed to this plan, and after making out a file card with all of this pertinent information, they began an excellent working relationship whereby Eileen could telephone ahead, explain her current needs, and make an appointment to try on clothes based on her existing wardrobe.

Navy/Green Working Capsule

	Colors			
	Navy	Green	Accents	Will work with
A. Jacket	Cardigan			All skirts
B. Jacket		Blazer		All skirts
C. Skirt	Pleated			All jackets, blouses and sweaters
D. Skirt		Pleated print Navy/green		All jackets, blouses and sweaters
E. Skirt	Slim knit			All jackets, blouses and sweaters
F. Jacket			White	All jackets, blouses and sweaters
G. Blouse			White	All skirts
H. Blouse		Print bow Navy/Green		All skirts
I. Blouse	Bow neck			All skirts
J. Sweater			Ivory pullover	All skirts
K. Sweater	Cardigan			
L. Dress		Shirtdress		
Accessories				
Shoes	Pumps			
Handbag	Envelope			
Earrings				Gold

THE PROBLEM

Every time Sandy G. went shopping, she found she was overwhelmed by all the clothing she saw. In fact, she even found herself getting anxious at the thought of going shopping. Inside the stores, the merchandise became bewildering and all began to look alike. When a salesperson approached her, she was unsure of what she wanted. If she tried things on, nothing seemed to look right. She would buy things out of frustration and anger. At home, her clothes never seemed to go together, but the idea of going shopping to find what she needed would just upset her again.

THE SOLUTION

Sandy and I took a morning and sorted through her closet, deciding what clothes she really liked and what she didn't. We removed the rejects from the closet and Sandy vowed to give them to friends or charity or put them on consignment in a second-hand store. We arranged what remained in her closet by color and found that most of her favorite clothes were beige or black. She also had some pieces in wine that she liked. We decided to work her clothes into a black and beige Capsule, using wine as an accent. She found that by looking at each piece of clothing on its own and trying it with the other items, she could create a lot of outfits. But what she really found she needed was two blouses, a white one and a beige one.

Setting out to go shopping, Sandy knew exactly what to look for in the store. She headed straight for the department that carried her price range in blouses, and zeroed in on what she needed. By doing this, Sandy was able to overcome her fear and she felt satisfied by the shopping experience. And for $80, Sandy was able to pull together a working wardrobe.

Black/Beige Working Capsule

	Colors			Will work with
	Black	**Beige**	**Accents**	
A. Jacket	Blazer			All skirts
B. Jacket		Tweed cardigan Black/beige		All skirts
C. Jacket		Blazer		All skirts
D. Skirt	Pleated			All jackets, blouses, and sweater
E. Skirt		Dirndl		All jackets, blouses, and sweater
F. Skirts		Wine	Pleated	All jackets, blouses and sweater
G. Skirt	A line			All jackets, blouses and sweater
H. Blouse	Shirt			All skirts
I. Blouse	Print shirt Black/beige			All skirts
J. Blouse			White shirt	All skirts
K. Blouse		Shirt		All skirts
L. Sweater			Wine pullover	All skirts

MAKING YOUR SELECTIONS

Once you find the departments in which you want to concentrate, you're ready for the third step—buying your clothes. Look carefully at the selection. If you see a skirt you like, carry it around the department and try to find other pieces that relate to it. Or, if you are trying to complete a Capsule by adding pieces to those you already own, bring along one or two of the items you already have in your closet. It is much easier to work with colors and shapes if you can see them in front of you rather than trying to remember what they look like. The mind's eye can play funny tricks, and what you remembered as a dark blue skirt may turn out to be three shades lighter.

Going into the dressing room presents a traumatic situation for many women. It is a place of confrontation with yourself, and the meeting can be unsettling if you aren't happy with what you see in the mirror. But it also can be a starting point, the time when you resolve to go on a diet or do those thigh-slimming exercises on a more consistent basis. The dressing room can also be the place where you can play with different looks, sample new colors, and experiment with the latest fashions. It is a private spot where you are free to try out a new role and see how it suits you.

Dressing rooms are notorious for evil mirrors and fading lightbulbs that seem to pick up everything that's wrong with your figure and little that's right. So when something looks good on you in the dressing room, you know it will look great on you in real life. If you have any doubts about the way an outfit looks, take it out to the selling floor and find a three-way mirror in good light; this will give you a true idea of how you look from every angle. One of the keys to dressing well is making sure you look attractive from the front, back, and side.

While you are looking in the mirror, ask yourself some questions. Is the skirt or dress a flattering length for you? Does it make you bulge in the wrong places? Is the shape too full or overpowering? Does the color complement your skin tone? Does it drain color from your face or add color to it? If the fabric is a print, is the pattern so large that it envelopes you, or is it small and neat enough that it works almost like a solid?

One important thing to look for is pockets, so that you, like your male counterpart, have a comfortable place to put your hands. Pockets can relieve a lot of the awkwardness many feel when they are standing and talking. Because pockets are an added expense for a manufacturer, they are often omitted in less expensive clothes but they are worth a few extra dollars to you if they help put you at ease.

When you are trying on a jacket, look carefully at its length. Does it cover your hips or end just in the middle of them? Midhip-length jackets make you look wider. Where does the jacket hit you·at the rear? Does it emphasize your derriere? If the jacket has pockets, do these conflict with the pockets on your skirt or dress, or does it cover them so that they don't fight one another? If the jacket is short, does it cover your waist, or does your blouse show?

If you are trying on a blouse, make sure it is long enough to be tucked neatly into your skirt. Are the sleeves long enough? On the other hand, are the sleeves too long and sloppy looking? Do the shoulders fit properly? Is the neckline flattering? Does it have a collar that can be worn in more than one way—up and down, button or unbuttoned? This kind of collar will give you much more versatility.

What about your own figure type? If you are short and slim, look for clothes that emphasize your tiny figure. You can wear tucks and pleats and carry off the very feminine details that many larger women cannot. If you're heavy or stocky, you can look slimmer and longer in clothes that are monotones. If you are narrow on top and broad through the hips, look for jackets and tops with shoulder pads or tucking at the shoulders. The extra width at the top will de-emphasize the bottom. If you are lucky enough to be tall, enjoy it. Not only can you carry off more extremes in fashion, you can also wear simple clothes with elegance and sophistication.

When it comes to trying on clothes, Nancy Kissinger has some good advice. Although she has learned a great deal from the American designers whose clothes she wears, her mother was her best teacher. "I have a fantastic mother who taught me about fit and things like that. She was also honest about what looked awful on me," Nancy says. Like any young girl, the tall, lanky Nancy did not always see herself the way others did. "I used to say, 'oh it's beautiful' and mother would say, 'yes, it's perfectly lovely, but it looks dreadful on you!' That sort of made you look at yourself realistically. So I'd say, 'yes, it's a perfectly beautiful dress. If I were five feet two and weighed ninety two pounds, it would look absolutely exquisite. But not at my height and weight."

While you are trying on clothes, think about how you can develop your own style. If there is someone you would like to emulate, consider whether she would wear this kind of look. If something in a fashion magazine has caught your eye, now is the time to try it on. It may look odd once you get it on, but then again it may open up a whole avenue of ideas. Accepting new ideas in fashion is a question of adapting your eye to change. Professionals in the fashion industry are used to seeing new ideas every season. Keep an open mind when it comes to new lengths, new shapes, and new color combinations. Then let your imagination roam so that you can come up with a look that will work for you.

While you are in the dressing room, play with the clothes you've selected. Try on different tops with different bottoms and see which combinations work and which don't. A good salesperson can help you here, but, unfortunately, you can't always depend on one being available so you must learn to do it yourself. If you've taken five things into the room and only one item works, discard what you don't want and go back to the selling floor with the one piece you like. Look for separates that will complement it. You may find that a wonderful sweater or a blouse in a new color can be just the catalyst your Capsule needs. The more complementary pieces you can find in one session, the easier your shopping will be.

THE PERFECT FIT

Good fit is terribly important and makes a major difference in how you look in your clothes. To get the best fit, you have to ignore sizes. It doesn't matter that your skirt is a size fourteen and your jacket is a size eight. Often two skirts will fit you well, one a size ten and the other a size twelve. You should realize that different manufacturers use different patterns for their sizing. Besides, it really doesn't matter what size you wear if you look good in the garment. No one is going to look at you as you walk in a room and think, "Gee, she looks good, but too bad her skirt is a size fourteen." They won't know and they won't care. All they will notice is your overall look.

If you find that the clothes you purchase do fit but need some adjustments, make sure you get them altered. For some women, there is a stigma attached to alterations, but there shouldn't be. Your figure is yours alone, but the clothes you are trying on were made for thousands of women. Therefore it stands to reason that it's almost impossible to achieve a perfect fit without some alterations. With a few adjustments, the suit or dress can look as if it were custom made. In some stores, the alterations woman can fit you on the spot, right in the dressing room. That way you know that when you get the clothing home, it will be ready to wear. Or perhaps the garment needs only minor adjustments that she can show you how to do yourself. Sometimes she will pin a hem for you and you can do the final sewing when you get home.

THE BEST TIME TO BUY

If you are just beginning to build your wardrobe, you might want to do your shopping when merchandise is at its peak in the stores. For most retailers, the year begins with January inventories and sales. Then slowly, in February, spring merchandise begins coming in. By March the departments are filling up, and this is a good time to do spring shopping. In April some of the earlier selections will go on sale as the summer stock begins to arrive. May is the peak time for summer clothes buying. After July Fourth, inventory comes again and with it the sales. Then at the end of July and in August, fall merchandise is on its way in; this is the time to take advantage of the best selection and newest styles. Dressy holiday clothes arrive in October and November, followed by resort wear in December and January.

The dream, of course, is to find everything you need in one department—and all of it on sale. That can happen sometimes, and I've seen it. I've even helped people put together entire Capsules from the markdown racks, but that is unusual. Sales, however, can be a great place to find what you need, especially if you know exactly what you are looking for. They can be expensive if you don't.

Most stores have sales at regularly scheduled times: fall clothing gets marked down after Thanksgiving; holiday clothes are reduced after the first of the year (usually after inventory); spring items go on sale after Easter; and summer clothes are marked down after the Fourth of July (again, usually after inventory). In between there are usually special reductions, such as Election Day coat sales, and during the course of the year there are always special purchases. Take advantage of your favorite store's promotional efforts. You'll be paying less money for regular merchandise. But make sure the item you're buying is really what you want, and that you are not buying it just because it is on sale. A bargain is a bargain only if you wear it and enjoy it; otherwise it can be another costly error. In shopping, learning to say no is as important as learning to say yes.

REAL PEOPLE

Mary DiGiacomo

Mary DiGiacomo is a banker who feels her clothing can be a definite asset. While her office in the International department of Manufacturers Hanover Trust sits high above Park Avenue, she does her shopping down on New York's Lower East Side. "I look for ideas on Fifth Avenue," she told me, but I shop at the discount stores around Canal Street twice a year." I buy very good things there." She wears suits, "because they project a good, clean business image," and also, she adds, "because they look good on me." She keeps her Capsule colors to black and beige, insists on natural fibers, and shops with an eye "for quality in fabric and cut." Choosing wool gabardine or wool crepe for her jackets and skirts, and silk for her blouses, she requires her jackets to be very well cut and tailored, and the skirts to move well. "I like my skirts to have pleats," says this five foot ten inch executive. "This makes them move better and look better on me." Her standard uniform is a silk blouse, a skirt and a jacket or sweater.

Like any smart investor, she watches her money and makes sure she gets a good return on it. "I take very good care of my clothes," she says. "That way they last a long time. I wear some things four and five years." She sends her clothes to a very good dry cleaner, giving them her blouses constantly, but her suits less frequently. The less dry cleaning, the longer the wools will last. "Even my shoes," she goes on, "I take them to the shoemaker as soon as I buy them. I have taps put on the front to protect them and I change the heels to German ones that never wear out. Then I put a cream on them for extra protection."

In the banker's tradition, Mary states, "I invest in my clothes." Her attitude is strictly business-like, but she never forgets she is a woman. "I think my femininity is my biggest asset," she says, "so why downplay it? You have to strike a happy medium between a professional stance and being a woman."

 Mary DiGiacamo: Working Capsule

Colors—Black/Beige

Fabrics—Silks, Wool gabardine, Wool crepe, Fibranne. Must be natural fibers.

Accessories—Watch: leather band for day, diamond and gold for evening. Thin gold chain. Pearls. Diamond studs or gold ball earrings.

Style—Suits. Silk shirts. Classic, Conservative, Elegant.

Key words—Fit. Cut. Investment.

Gail Serfaty

Gail Serfaty is one working woman who always prefers to wear dresses, but she gives them a special touch. "As soon as I buy my clothes, I make changes," says the assistant curator of the State Department. "I buy mostly dresses, and I'll often change all of the buttons. Or I may take off a collar and put on an old lace one. Or add a silk flower, or change a belt. That way I give them their own look." She chooses dark colored clothes that are pretty but practical, working around a color scheme of navy and beige. She prefers dresses that have wide sleeves so she can move her arms easily, and full skirts so she can bend without any problems. Her favorite fabrics have the look of silk but are made of synthetics that are crease-resistant and washable. For business meetings, she'll often slip on a jacket or cardigan sweater to give her dress an even more finished look.

When she shops, which is three or four times a year, she heads for the better stores and buys most of her things on sale. "I look for quality and for classic styling," she says. "And I find that better clothes are styled to stay in fashion longer."

SHOPPING WITH A PLAN

The following budget offers a guideline for comparison of designer, better and moderate priced clothing. Please note that prices may vary from season to season.

The manufacturers listed represent some of the names in each category.

Designer	Better	Moderate
Anne Klein	Ciao	Century
Betty Hanson	Devon Hall	Chaus
Blassport	Diane Von Furstenberg	College-Town
Calvin Klein	Evan Picone	Evelyn De Jonge
Friedericks Sport	Finity	Koret
Harve Bernard	J. G. Hook	Lady Manhattan
Kasper for J. L. Sport	Jack Mulqueen	Regatta Sport
Kasper for Joan Leslie	Jones	Schrader Sport
Nipon Boutique	Liz Claiborne	Summit
Stanley Blacker	Marisa Christina	Yves Jennet

Budgeting A Capsule

	Designer	Better	Moderate	Your Capsule
Jacket	$ 175	$120	$ 85	
Jacket	210	125	95	
Skirt	125	60	45	
Skirt	105	68	40	
Skirt	110	45	38	
Blouse	90	35	30	
Blouse	110	40	25	
Blouse	80	46	29	
Blouse	120	42	28	
Sweater	175	70	37	
Sweater	140	75	32	
Dress	250	98	60	
TOTAL	$1,690	$824	$545	

Whether you shop on your own or with someone else's guidance, be sure to take along a personal checklist provided at the end of this chapter. This checklist enumerates the twelve pieces you need for a working wardrobe Capsule: two jackets, three skirts, four blouses, two sweaters, and one dress. To get an approximate idea of what these twelve pieces might cost, see the Budgeting A Capsule chart. Remember, these twelve pieces will enable you to make at least forty different outfits, but you must keep to the two colors of your Capsule and work with compatible shapes. You might even take along a chart for one of the Capsules featured in Chapter 1. It will give you a good guideline to follow.

Before you buy anything, ask yourself these five important questions:

1. Is it in my Capsule colors?

2. Will it work with the other pieces in my Capsule?

3. Is it flattering to me?

4. Is it well made so that it will last?

5. Will it help me project the look I want for myself?

If you can answer yes to these questions, you will be on your way to constructing cohesive Capsules, and you will be building your own working wardrobe.

Wardrobe Checklist

Capsule Colors: _____/_____

	Have	Need	Color	Description	Will work with
Jacket					
Jacket					
Skirt					
Skirt					
Skirt					
Blouse					
Blouse					
Blouse					
Blouse					
Sweater					
Sweater					
Dress					
Coat					

Acessories Checklist

Capsule Colors: _____/_____

	Have	Need	Color	Description	Will work with
Shoes					
Shoes					
Handbag					
Briefcase					
Belt					
Belt					
Scarf					
Scarf					
Scarf					
Watch					
Earrings					
Earrings					
Necklace					
Necklace					
Bracelet					

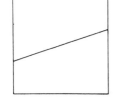

Chapter 7

FINDING YOUR INDIVIDUAL STYLE

The Capsule Concept can be applied to your wardrobe, no matter what your personal style. But it *is* important to develop a style of your own. Not only does that give you a signature, but it also affords you an easy approach to shopping. Once you know your own look, you can save time and money by heading just for the looks that say "you." I watched a well dressed man one day trying on coats in a department store. One after another, he tried them on, looked at himself in the mirror, and then rejected them, remarking to his companion, "It didn't say 'hello'." When you know what your very own look is, you will recognize it at once when you try it on, and it will, indeed, say "hello."

To simplify styles of dress, I have divided looks into four categories: the Romantic, the Pragmatist, the Individualist, and the Modernist.

The Romantic adores flowered patterns and flowing, graceful styles. When she buys a blouse it tends to have ruffles, pleats, embroidery or some extra detail of femininity. Her skirts are full, her hair soft, and her accessories flowers and cameos. She pictures herself as a girl on a hill in a Renoir painting or as Scarlett O'Hara in Gone With the Wind. She might choose a career as a ballerina, a poet or an actress. The Romantic might wear the Capsule on page 19, jacket B—Blouse G—Skirt E.

The Pragmatist feels comfortable with practical, versatile clothes with classic tailoring. Her blouses might have convertible collars, her jackets are usually blazers, and her skirts are modified in their slimness. If she wears prints, they are geometrics or paisleys. If she wears any accessories, they are the basics. She identified with the role of Faye Dunaway in the movie, Network, and if she were in a movie, a play, or the corporate world, she'd be the Woman of the Year. Executive, lawyer or banker are the careers she might choose. She'd likely wear the pieces on page 19, dress L and jacket C, to reflect her business image.

The Individualist prefers fashions that are simple enough to carry off her favorite accessories and give her a totally unique look. Her blouses may be collarless so that she can wear different scarves or unusual necklaces. She tends to solid colors to set off her favorite acquisitions, and she may choose one color or one accent as her signature. If she were a dancer, she would admire Isadora Duncan, if she were an artist, Louise Nevelson, and as a fashion leader, Diana Vreeland. A painter, a writer, or a chef would be her choice for a career. The Individualist would be comfortable in the Capsule on page 19, jacket A—sweater K—blouse I—skirt D.

The Modernist takes a contemporary approach to her clothing, preferring looks that are fashion forward. She enjoys seeing the trends in fashion magazines, and likes to experiment with the ideas of designers. She may pad her shoulders, belt her jackets, wrap her waist to give her clothing the latest look, or experiment with color. She may see herself as the contemporary woman in the ads for Virginia Slims, as a fashion model from the pages of Vogue or Bazaar, or even as the fashion photographer, like the title role in Eyes of Laura Mars. She's likely to wear Jacket C—blouse J—skirt F from the Capsule on page 19.

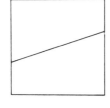

Chapter 8

PLANNING YOUR CAPSULE

The Capsule Concept provides flexibility so that you have as many pieces in each category (skirts, pants, jackets, blouses, sweaters, dresses) as you like. While one twelve piece Capsule may have one jacket, another may include two, and another may have three. One Capsule may have only skirts, while another may include pants. Your Capsules should reflect your preferences. A variety of charts have been included in this Chapter so that you may work out different Capsules based on your own needs.

_____ / _____ **Working Capsule**

	Colors		
		Accents	Will work with
A.			
B.			
C.			
D.			
E.			
F.			
G.			
H.			
I.			
J.			
K.			
L.			

Accessories

_____ / _____ # Working Capsule

	Colors		Accents	Will work with
A.				
B.				
C.				
D.				
E.				
F.				
G.				
H.				
I.				
J.				
K.				
L.				

Accessories

_____ / _____ **Evening Capsule**

	Colors		Accents	Will work with
A.				
B.				
C.				
D.				
E.				
F.				
G.				
H.				
I.				

Accessories

Travel Capsule

Three Day Trip

		Accents	Will work with
Jacket			
Skirt			
Skirt			
Skirt			
Blouse			
Blouse			
Dress			

Checklist

	Robe (Lightweight)
	Sleepwear
	Underwear
	Cosmetics
	Hair dryer
	Travel curlers
	Hand steamer
	Medicine
	Sports equipment

Accessories

Shoes			
Handbag			
Belts			
Scarves			
Watch			
Earrings			
Necklace			
Bracelet			

_____ / _____ Travel Capsule
One-Week Convention

			Accents	Will work with
Jacket				
Jacket				
Skirt				
Skirt				
Pants				
Blouse				
Blouse				
Blouse				
Sweater				
Dress				
Active wear				
Active wear				

Checklist

	Robe (Lightweight)
	Sleepwear
	Underwear
	Cosmetics
	Hair dryer
	Travel curlers
	Hand steamer
	Medicine
	Sports equipment

Accessories

Shoes			
Handbag			
Belts			
Scarves			
Watch			
Earrings			
Necklace			
Bracelet			

_____ / _____ **Capsule**

Essential Accessories

			Accents
Shoes			
Handbag			
Briefcase			
Belts			
Scarves*			
Watch			
Earrings			
Necklace			
Bracelet			

*See illustrations on ways to tie a scarf.

INDEX

IMPORTANT BOOKS
FOR YOUR CAREER

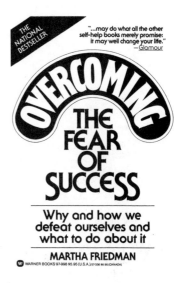

OVERCOMING THE FEAR OF SUCCESS
**Why and How We Defeat Ourselves and
What to Do About It**

by Martha Friedman

- Are you always late, no matter
  how hard you try to be on time?
- Are you a perfectionist?
- Do you procrastinate?
- Do you fear intimacy or closeness?

If you said *yes* to any of these questions, chances are you have a fear of success. Psychotherapist Martha Friedman tells us in plain language how we unconsciously sabotage our chances for success, how to recognize and overcome our hidden fears, and how to discover true fulfillment in love, work, and play. It's all right here!

Available in Large-Size Quality Paperback   (J97-998, $5.95, U.S.A.)
(J37-336, $6.95, Canada)

NEW FROM WARNER BOOKS

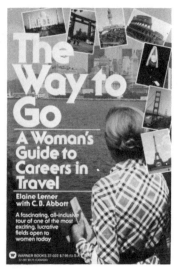

THE WAY TO GO:
A WOMAN'S GUIDE TO CAREERS IN TRAVEL

by Elaine Lerner with C. B. Abbott

This book will help you further your career growth by giving you:

• Invaluable information on how to break into the field, including facts on training programs and airline schools, plus job descriptions of beginner positions in travel agencies, hotels, the airlines, and more

• Tips and advice on moving up to success—checklists of personality traits necessary for the field and its different branches, plus how-tos on climbing the executive ladder and overcoming sexism

• A thorough description of the jobs and opportunities and the various "ways to go": Tour Operating, Airline Sales, Meeting and Convention Travel, Hotel Sales, Incentive Travel, as well as Opening Your Own Agency—where the big money is, where the great travel discounts are, and where the market is wide open for women!

Find out about the perks, quirks, prerequisites, and outstanding rewards of the travel business: *The Way to Go* is your highly informative guide to success!